Theodore de Beze, William Crashaw

The Italian convert

News from Italy of a second Moses

Theodore de Beze, William Crashaw

The Italian convert
News from Italy of a second Moses

ISBN/EAN: 9783337102302

Printed in Europe, USA, Canada, Australia, Japan

Cover: Foto ©ninafisch / pixelio.de

More available books at **www.hansebooks.com**

THE Italian Convert:

NEWS from *ITALY* of a Second

MOSES:

Or the LIFE of

Galeacius Caracciolus,

The Noble Marquess of *Vico*.

Containing the Story of his Admirable Conversion from Popery, and forsaking of a rich Marquesdom for the Gospels sake.

Illustrated with several Figures.

Written first in *Italian*, thence translated into Latin by Reverend *BEZA*; and for the benefit of our people put into English: And now published

By *W. C.*

In memoria sempiterna Justus.

Psalm 112. *The Just shall be had in everlasting remembrance.*

London, Printed for *Abel Roper*, at the Sign of the Sun in *Fleetstreet* against St. *Dunstans* Church, 1677

TO THE RIGHT HONOURABLE,

And my very good Lord,

EDMUND Lord SHEFFEILD,

Lord Lieutenant in the North, and Lord President of His Highnes Council there ; of the Noble Order of the Garter.

And to the Right Honourable and Religious Ladies, the Lady *Dowglass* his Mother, and Lady *Ursula* his Wife, and to all the vertuous offspring of that Noble Race, Grace and Peace, &c

GIVE me leave (Right Honourable) to put you all in one Epistle, whom God and nature hath linked so well together: Nature in the nearest bond, and God in the holiest Religion. For a simple New-years-Gift, I present you with as strange a story, as (out of the holy stories) was ever heard. Will your Honours have the whole in brief, afore it be laid down at large. Thus it is:

Galeacius.

The Epistle

Galeacius Carracciolus, *son and heir apparent to* Calantonius *Marquess of* Vicum *in* Naples, *bred, born, and brought up in Popery, a Courtier to* Charles *the fifth, Nephew to the Pope* Paul *the fourth, being married to the Duke of* Nucernes's *Daughter, and having by her six goodly Children, at a Sermon of* Peter Martyrs, *was first touched; after by reading Scripture, and other good means, was fully converted; laboured with his Lady, but could not perswade her. Therefore that he might enjoy Christ, and serve him with a quiet conscience, he left the Lands, Livings, and Honours of a Marquesdome, the comforts of his Lady and Children, the pleasures of* Italy, *his credit with the Emperour, his kindred with the Pope, and forsaking all for the love of Jesus Christ, came to* Geneva, *and there lived a poor and mean, but yet an honourable and an holy life, for forty years. And though his Father, his Lady, his Kinsmen, yea, the Emperour, and the Pope, did all they could to reclaim him, yet continued he constant to the end, and lived and dyed the blessed servant of God, leaving behind him a rare example to all Ages.*

This (Right Honourable) is a Brief of the whole, and it is a story admirable and imitable of any other in this latter age of the World. Some

Dedicatory.

Some use to crave of great personages, not to respect the gift, but the giver; but in this case I contrariwise entreat your Honors, not to respect the giver, but the gift: of the giver I say enough, if I say nothing: but of the gift, I mean of noble *Galeacius*, I say too little when I have said all I can. But this I must needs say, so religious, so noble, so vertuous was the man; so resolute, so holy, so heroical was the fact, so strange the beginning, so admirable and extraordinary the perseverance, as if the story were not debased by the rudeness of my translation, I durst say, none so great but might read it, nor so good but might follow it. I may say much rather than *Jacob; few and evil have my days been*; Yet in these few days of mine something have I seen; more have I read; more have I heard; yet never saw I, heard I, or read I any example (all things laid together) more nearly seconding the example of *Moses*, than this, of this most renowned Marquess *Galeacius*. *Moses* was the adopted Son of a Kings daughter; *Galeacius* the natural Son and Heir apparent to a Marquess: *Moses* a Courtier, in the Court of *Pharaoh*: *Galeacius* in the Court of the Emperor *Charles* the fifth: *Moses* by adoption a kin to a Queen; *Galeacius* by marrige a kin to a Duke: by blood, son to a Marquess, Nephew to a Pope:

The Epistle.

Moses in possibility of a Kingdom; he in possession of a Marquesdom: *Moses* in his youth brought up in the heathenism of *Egypt*; *Galeacius* noozeled in the superstition of Popery: *Moses* at last saw the truth and embraced it, so did *Galeacius*: *Moses* openly fell from the heathenism of *Egypt*, so did *Galeacius* from the superstition of Popery. But all this is nothing to that which they both suffered for their conscience. What *Moses* suffered St. *Paul* tells us; Moses *when he was come to years, refused to be called the son of* Pharaoh's *daughter, and chose rather to suffer adversity with the people of God, than to enjoy the pleasures of sin for a season; esteeming the rebuke of Christ greater riches than the treasures of* Egypt: Nay, *Moses* had rather be a base brick-maker among the oppressed *Israelites*, being true Christians, than to be the son of a King's daughter in the Court of *Pharaoh* amongst Idolaters. In like case Noble *Galeacius*, when he was come to years and knowledge of Christ, refused to be called son and heir to a Marquess, Cup-bearer to an Emperour, Nephew to a Pope; and chose rather to suffer affliction, persecution, banishment, loss of Lands, Livings, Wife, Children, Honours and Preferments, than to enjoy the sinfull pleasures of *Italy* for a season, esteeming the

Dedicatory.

the rebuke of Christ greater riches than the honours of a Marquesdom without Christ; and therefore seeing he must either want Christ, or want them, he dispoiled himself of all these to gain Christ.

If (Right Honourable) the wise fools of this world might have the censuring of these two men and their actions, they would presently judge them a couple of impassionate and stoical fellows, or else melancholick & brain-sick men, to refuse Marquesdoms and Kingdoms for scruple of conscience: but no matter as long as the men are Saints in Heaven, and their actions honoured of God and his Angels; admired of good men, and neglected of none but those, who as they will not follow them on earth, so are they sure never to follow them to heaven. So excellent was the fact of *Moses,* and so heroical, that the Holy Ghost vouchsafes it remembrance, both in the Old and New Testament, that so the Church in all ages might know it and admire it: and doth chronicle it in the Epistle to the *Hebrews* almost 2000 years after it was done. If God himself did so to *Moses,* shall not God's Church be carefull to commend to posterity this second *Moses,* whose love to Christ Jesus was so zealous, and so inflamed by the heavenly fire of God's Spirit, that no earthly

temptations

temptations could either quench or abate it; but to win Chrift, & to enjoy him in the liberty of his Word and Sacraments, he delicately contemned the honours and pleafures of the Marquefdom of *Vicum*. *Vicum*, one of the Paradices of. *Naples*, *Naples* the Paradice of *Italy*: *Italy* of *Europe* : *Europe* of the Earth : yet all thefe Paradices were nothing to him in comparifon of attaining the celeftial Paradife, there to live with Jefus Chrift.

If any Papifts (mufing, as they ufe and meafuring us by themfelves) do fufpect the ftory to be fome feigned thing, devifed to allure & entice the peoples minds, and to fet a flourifh upon our Religion, as they be a thoufand falfe and feigned ftories and miracles ufe to do. I anfwer, firft in the general, far be it from us & our Religion to ufe fuch means, either for our felves, or againft our adverfaries : no, we are content the Church of *Rome* have the glory of that Garland. Popery being a fandy, and a fhaken, a rotten & a tottering building, needs fuch props to under-fet it: but truth dare fhew her felf, & fears no colours. But for the particular, I anfwer; cunning liars (as many Monks were) fram'd their tales of men that lived long ago, and places afar off and unknown; that fo their reports may not too eafily be brought to trial. But in this cafe it is far otherwife;
the

Dedicatory.

he circumstances are notorious; the persons and places famously known: *Vicum, Naples, Italy, Geneva*, are places well known: *Calantonius* his father, *Charles* the fifth, his Lord & Master, Pope *Paul* the fourth his Uncle, were persons well known: examine either places or persons, and spare none; Truth seeks no corners; disprove the story who can, we crave no sparing; neither is the time too far past, but may soon be examined. He was born within these two hundred years, and died at *Geneva*, and his sons son at this day is Marquess of *Vicum*. Let any Papist do what he can, he shall have more comfort in following the example, than credit in seeking to disprove the story.

In the course of my poor reading, (Right Honourable) I have often found mention of this noble Marq. & of his strange conversion; but the story it self, I first found it in the exquisite Library of the good Gent. Mr. *Gee*, one that honors learning in others, and cherisheth it in himself: and having not once read it, but often perused it, I thought it great loss to our Church to want so rare a Jewel; and therefore could not but take the benefit of some stoln hours to put the same into our Tongue, for the benefit of my brethren in this Realm, who want knowledg in the *Italian* and *Latine* Tongues. And now being translated, I humbly offer

offer and confecrate it to my holy mother the Church of *England*, who may rejoyce to fee her Religion fpreading her felf privily in the heart of *Italy*; and to fee the Popes Nephew become her Son. And next of all unto you (Right Honourable) to whom I am bound in fo many bonds of duty, and to whom this ftory doth fo fitly appertain. You (my Honourable good Lord) may here fee a noble Gentleman of your own rank, in defcent, birth, education, advancements like your felf, to be like you alfo in the love and liking of the fame holy Religion. And you, good Madam, may here conceive and judge by your felf, how much more happy this Noble Marquefs had been, if his Lady Madam *Victoria* had been like your felf; I mean, if fhe had followed and accompanied her Lord in that his moft holy and happy converfion. And you all (Right Honourable) in this Noble Marquefs, as in a cryftal-glafs, may behold your felves, of whom I hope you will give me leave to fpeak (that which to the great glory of God you fpare not to fpeak of your felves) that you were once darknefs, but now are light in the Lord: Bleffed be that God the father of light, whofe glorious light hath fhined in your hearts. Behold (Right Honourable) you are not alone; behold an *Italian*; behold a noble Marquefs hath broken the ice; and trodden

Dedicatory:

en the path before you. In him you may see that God's Religion is as well in *Italy* as in *England*: I mean, that though the face of *Italy* be the seat of *Antichrist*, yet in the heart thereof is a remnant of the Lord of Hosts.

You may see this Noble Marquess in this story now after his death, whom in his lifetime so many Noble Princes desired to see. His body lies in the bowels of the earth, but his soul lives in Heaven in the bosom of Jesus Christ, and his Religion in your hearts, and his name shall live for every in this story. Accept it therefore (Right Honourable) & if for my sake you wil vouchsafe to read it once over, I dare say, that afterwards for your own sake you wil read it over and over again, which if you do, you shall find it will stir up your pure minds, and inflame your hearts with a yet more earnest zeal to the truth, and will be an affectual means to encrease your faith, your fear of God, your humility, patience, constancy, and all other vertues of Regeneration. And for my part, I freely and truly profess, I have bin oft ravisht with admiration of this noble example, to see an *Italian* so excellent a Christian, one so near the Pope, so near to Jesus Christ; and such blessed fruit to blossom in the Popes own garden, and to see a Nobleman of *Italy*, forsake that for Christ, for which I fear

many

The Epistle

many amongst us would forsake Christ himself, and surely (I confess truth) the serious consideration of this so late, so true, so strange an Example, hath been a spur to my slowness, and whetted my dull spirits, and made me esteem more highly of Religion than I did before. I know it is an accusation of my self, and a disclosing of my own shame to confess thus much, but it is a glory to God, an honour to Religion, a credit to the Truth, & a praise to this noble Marquess, & therefore I will not hide it.

And why should I shame to confess it, when that famous and renowned man of God, holy *Calvin* freely confesseth, (as in the sequel of this story you shall hear) that this Noblemans Example did greatly confirm him in his Religion, and did revive, strengthen his faith, and cheer up all the holy Graces of God in him? And surely (most worthy Lord, and honorable Ladies) this cannot but confirm and comfort you in your holy courses, and as it were put a new life unto the Graces of God in you, when you see, what? not the common people, but even such as were like your selves, have suffred for Religion? and when you see, that not only the poor and baser sort of men, but even the mighty and honourable (as your selves are) do think themselves honoured by embracing Religion. Pardon my plainness, and too much bold-

Dedicatory.

boldness with your Honors, and vouchsafe to accept it as proceeding from one who much tendreth your Salvations, and rejoyceth with many thousands more, to behold the mighty & gracious work of God in you. Go forward Noble Lord, in the Name of the Lord of host, still to honor that honourable place you hold, still to defeat the vain expectation of Gods enemies; and to satisfie the godly hopes & desires of holy men: still to discountenance Popery & all prophaness: still by your personal diligence in frequenting holy exercises, to bring on that backward City: by your godly discipline in your Family, to reform or to condemn the dissoluteness & disorder of the most great Families in this Country: still to minister justice without delay, to cut up contentions, & save the Lawyers labour: still to relieve the fatherless and the Widow, and help the poor against their oppressors: and which is all in all, still to subplant Superstition, Popery, Ignorance and wilfull blindness: and to plant and disperse true Religion in that City, and these Northern Countries. But all these means still shewing your self an holy & zealous *Phinehas* (under the great *Phinehas* our most worthy Soveraign) to execute Gods judgment, and to take vengeance on the *Zimri* & *Cozbi* of our Nation: namely, on Popery and Prophaneness,

the

The Epistle, &c.

the two great sins which have pull'd down God's plagues on our Land, and the due and zealous punishment whereof, will be the means to remove them.

But I wrong your Honours to trouble you with these my too many and too ragged lines: and I wrong this Noble Gentleman, to clothe his golden story with this my rude and home-spun English-stile; and I wrong you all to keep you so long from being acquainted with this Noble Marquess, so like your selves; at whose meeting and acquaintance I am sure there will be so much rejoycing, and mutual congratulation at the mighty and gracious work of God in you all. The same God and merciful Father I humbly beseech, and ever will, to accomplish his good work in you, as he did in that Noble Marquess: and as he hath already made you so many blessed, blessed in your selves, blessed one in another, blessed in your conversions, blessed above many, in your many and religious Children: so at last he may make you most of all blessed in your ends; that so after this life you may attain the eternal glory of a better world, whither this noble Marquess is gone before you.

Your Honours in all Christian duty,

W. C.

TO THE
Christian & Courteous
READERS.

GOOD *Reader, conceive I pray thee, that this translation being made divers years ago, and communicated to my private friends, I thought to have suppressed it from spreading further; but being pressed by importunity, and urged with unavoidable reasons, I have now yielded to let it pass in publick; the rather considering, that at this day almost every hour yields a new Book, yet many ages afford scarce one example like to this. I have divided it into Chapters for thy better ease in reading and remembring: and seeing I find*

The Epistle to the Reader.

in other Authours often mention of this Noble Marquess, and his heroical fact: I have therefore not tied my self precisely to the words of the Latin story, but keeping the sense and scope, have sometime inlarged my self as the circumstance seemed to require, or as I had warrant and direction from other stories. Read it with an holy and humble heart, and prayer to God, and account me thy Debter, if thou think not thy labour well bestowed. And when thou findest a blessing, and reapest spiritual comfort hereby, then vouchsafe to remember me in thy Prayers;

Thy Brother in Christ,

W. C.

Of the Lineage, Birth, and Infancy of GALEACIUS CARACCIOLUS, the Noble Marquess of *Vico*.

CHAPTER I.

My purpose is to commit to writing, the Life of Galeacius Caracciolus *: as being a rare example of a most strange & seldom seen constancy, in the defence of godliness & true Christian Religion.*

HE was born at *Naples*, a renowned City in *Italy*, in the month of *January*, in the year of Christ 1517. [*The very year when Luther began to preach the Gospel.*] His Fathers name was *Calantonius*, who was descended of the Ancient and Noble house of the *Caracciolies* in the Country of *Capua*. This *Calantonius*, even in his youth, was not only well respected, but highly

highly esteemed, and a familiar friend of that Noble Prince of *Orange*, who after the taking and sacking of *Rome*, was placed in the room of the Duke of *Burbon*: yea his faithfulness and industry was so well approved to the Prince (as oftentimes afore, so especially) at the siege of *Naples*, what time it was assaulted by *Lotrechins*, as that afterward, when the Emperour *Charles* the fifth of that name, (who then was at *Rome* to receive the Imperial Crown, and other Ornaments of the Empire) did appoint the said Prince with certain forces to go and besiege the City of *Florence*, he thought it needful to take the said *Calantonius* with him, for his wisdom and grave Counsel. From whence, when that service was ended, he being sent to *Cæsar* himself, he did so wisely demean himself in all his affairs, and did so sufficiently satisfie the Emperour in all things, that he made good in every point, that worthy testimony which the Prince had given of him, whereupon he, being at that time most honourably entertained of the Emperour himself, was by him not only advanced to the state and title of a Marquess, but also equally joyned in commission with the Viceroy of *Naples*, (for his wisdom and experience in all kind of affairs) to be assistant unto him, and fellow

low with him in swaying the Scepter of that Kingdom. In which office and function he so carried himself, as he won the good will of both small and great, as well of the Nobles, as of the Commonalty : yea insomuch as he was deeply invested in the favour of the Emperour *Charles*, and King *Phillip* his Son. And so he continued in this dignity, till the last day of his life, which was in the month of *February*, in the year 1562. he being himself more than threescore and ten years of age.

Such a father and no worse had this *Galeacius*. As for his Mother, she was descended of the Noble family of the *Caraffi* : and her own Brother was afterward Pope of *Rome* [*That is Pope* Paul *the fourth*.] Which I affirm, not to that end, as though this in it self was any true praise or honour to *Galeacius*, but that his love to true Religion, and his constancy in defence thereof (even against such mighty ones) may appear the more admirable to all that hear it, as it hereby did to all that knew him : Of which his love to true Religion, we shall speak more anon.

Galeacius being twenty years old, and the only son of his mother, who was now deceased ; his father *Calantonius* being desirous to continue his name, to preserve his house and posterity, and to maintain his estate and patrimony, whose lands amounted to the sum of five thousand pounds a year and upward; did therefore provide him a Wife, a Virgin of noble birth, called *Victoria*, daughter to the Duke of *Nuceria*, one of the principal Peers of *Italy*, with whom he had in name of portion or dowry six thousand five hundred pounds. He lived with his wife *Victoria* unto the year 1551. At which time he forsook house, family, and country for Religions sake: and in that time he had by his wife six children, (four sons and two daughters.) His eldest son died at *Panorma*, in the year 1577, leaving behind him one son and one daughter: the son obtaining by inheritance the Marquesdom of *Vicum*, (amongst divers other things) maried a wife of noble birth afore his Grandfather *Galeacius* died: by whom, as I hear, he hath two children, to whom this *Galeacius* is great Grandfather.

  Now all these particulars do I thus set down to this end, that the perseverance of so great a man may appear the better by all these circumstances, which is no less than a most glorious victory over so many temptations.

CHAP.

CHAP II.

Of his preferment at Court, and the first occasion of his conversion.

THe Marquess *Calantonius* seeing so good hope of the continuance of his house and posterity, desiring not to preserve only, but to increase and augment the dignity of his house, purposed therefore that his son *Galeacius* should seek further honour and follow the Court. Wherefore making offer of him to the Emperour *Charles*, he was most kindly entertained into the Emperors house and service, and soon after was made the Emperors Gentleman-sewer. In which place and office within short time, he both won the favour of the Nobility, and the rest of the Court, and grew to be of special account even with the Emperor himself: for all mens opinion and judgment of him was, that there was not one of many to be compared with him, for innocency of life, elegancy of manners, sound judgment, and knowledg of many things. Thus *Galeacius* was in all mens opinions in the high way to all honour and estimation: for the Prince whom he served

was

was most mighty & the Monarch of the biggest part of the Christian world. But all this was little: for God, the King of Kings, of his singular mercy and grace did purpose to call him to far greater dignity, and to more certain and durable riches. And this so great and rare a work did the Lord bring to pass, by strange and special means. So it was that in those days, a certain *Spaniard* a Nobleman did sojourn at *Naples,* who had to name *Johannes Waldesius*; this Gentleman being come to some knowledg of the truth of the Gospel, and especially of the Doctrine of Justification, used often to confer with, and to instruct divers other Noblemen, his Companions and familiars, in points of Religion, confuting the false opinions of our own inherent justification, and of the merits of good works, and so consequently detecting the vanity of many Popish points, and the fondness of their superstitions: by which means he so prevailed, or rather the Lord by him, that divers of these Noble Gentlemen began to creep out of Popish darkness, and to perceive some light of the truth: Amongst these was there one *Johannes Franciscus Cæsaria,* a Noble Gentleman and kinsman to this our *Galeacius.*

Of this Gentleman first of all did *Galeacius* hear

hear divers things in conference, which seemed to him much contrary to the course of the vain world; yea, much to cross even his age and estate, and course of life; as namely of the true means of our justification, of the excellency and power of Gods Word, of the vanity of the most of Popish superstitions, &c. For *Galeacius* esteemed and used this Gentleman as his familiar friend, both being near of his blood, & especially for that he was a Gentleman of very good parts. Now although the speeches of this Gentleman did not at the first so far prevail with him, as to make him forsake the vanities of this life; notwithstanding it was not altogether in vain: for that God which had ordained him to be a special instrument of his glory, would not suffer so good seed to perish, though it seemed for a time to be cast even amongst thorns: neither will it be beside the purpose to set down particularly the means which it pleased God to use for the working of this strange conversion: amongst which this was one.

CHAP. III.
Of the means of his further sanctification.

AT that time, *Peter Martyr Vermilius*, a *Florentine*, was a publick Preacher and Reader

Reader at *Naples*. This man was a Canon regular (as they call them) a man since then of great name for his singular knowledg in Christian religion, his godly manners and behaviours, and for his sweat and copious teaching; for he afterwards casting away his Monks Cowle, and renouncing the superstitions of Popery, he shon so brightly in Gods Church, that he dispersed and strangely drove away the darkness and mist of Popery. *Galeacius* was once content at *Cæsarta* his motion to be drawn to hear *Peter Martyrs* Sermon; yet not so much for any desire he had to learn, as moved and tickled with a curious humour to hear so famous a man as then *Martyr* was accounted. At that time *Peter Martyr* was in hand with *Pauls* first Epistle to the *Corinthians*, and as he was shewing the weakness and deceitfulness of the judgment of mans reason in spiritual things, as likewise the power and efficacy of the word of God in those men in whom the Lord worketh by his Spirit: amongst other things he used this Simile or Comparison: If a man walking in a large place, see afar off men and women dancing together, and hear no sound of Instrument, he will judg them mad, or at least foolish; but if he come nearer them, and perceive their order, and hear their Musick, and

and mark their measures and their courses, he will then be of another mind, and not only take delight in seeing them, but feel a desire in himself to bear them company and dance with them. Even the same (said *Martyr*) betides many men, who when they behold in others a sudden and great change of their looks, apparel, behaviour, and whole course of life, at the first sight they impute it to melancholy, or some other foolish humour; but if they look more narrowly into the matter, and begin to hear and perceive the harmony and sweet consent of Gods Spirit, and his Word in them, (by the joynt power of which two, this change was made and wrought, which afore they accounted folly) then they change their opinion of them, and first of all begin to like them, and that change in them, and afterward feel in themselves a motion and desire to imitate them, and to be of the number of such men, who forsaking the World and his vanities, do think that they ought to reform their lives by the rule of the Gospel, that so they may come to true and sound holiness. This comparison by the grace of Gods Spirit wrought so wonderfully with *Galeacius* (as himself hath often told his friends) that from that hour he resolv'd with himself, more carefully to restrain his affections from

following

following the world and his pleasures, as before they did, and to set his mind about seeking out the truth of Religion, and the way to true happiness.

[*See how the first step of a mans conversion from Popery is true and sound mortification of carnal lusts, and a change of life, See also how the first means to bring a man out of error to the truth, is study of holy Scriptures.*]

To this purpose, he began to read the Scriptures every day being perswaded, that truth of Religion, and soundness of wisdom, was to be drawn out of that fountain, and that the high way to heaven was thence to be sought. And further, all his acquaintance and familiarity did he turn into such company, as out of whose life and conferences he was perswaded he might reap the fruit of godliness and pure Religion. And thus far in this short time had the Lord wrought with him by that Sermon: as first, to consider whether he were right or no; secondly to take up a continual exercise of reading Scripture; thirdly, to change his former company, and make choice of better. And this was done in the year 1541. and in the four and twentieth year of his age.

CHAP.

CHAP. IV.

Of the strange censures the World gave of his conversion, and how the better sort rejoyced at it.

BUT when this sudden alteration of this Noble and young *Galeacius* was seen and perceived in *Naples*, it can be scarce set down how greatly it amazed his companions; which as yet cleaved to the world and to the affections of the flesh: many of them able to render no cause of it, could not tell what to say of it: some judged it but a malancholick passion: others thought it plain folly, and fearing he would become simple and doting, and that his wit began by some means to be empaired. Thus every one gave his verdict and censure of him, but all wondred, and doubted what it would turn to. But the better sort of men, and such as feared God, and had their mind inlightned with some knowledg of Religion, as they wondred no less to see so great a change in so great a man, so likewise they were surprized with exceeding joy to see it: for they were persivaded, that God had some great and extraordinary work
in

in it ? that a young Gallant, a Noble man of such wealth and honour as he was, living in such delight and pleasures, in so general a corruption of life, both in Court and Countrey, but especially his age, nobility, wealth, and honour being joyned with the wanton deliciousness of the Courtly life: I say, that such a man should be indued with the spirit of holiness, and so far affected with Repentance, as that he should contemn all those in respect of Heaven; they esteemed of it (as it was indeed) a rare matter, and seldom seen in the world: and therefore they greatly rejoyced at it, and praised the Lord on his behalf. Amongst those men that thus rejoyced at his conversion, was one *Marcus Antonius Flaminius*, a Scholar of great name, and an excellent Poet, as his Paraphrase on the *Psalms*, and other very good Poems do sufficiently testify. *Galeacius* about this time received a Letter from this *Flaminius*; wherein he did congratulate, & rejoyce with him, for the grace and gift of God, which was bestowed on him in his conversion. This Letter I thought good to insert into the body of this story, (as being worthy of no less) to the end that it might be a witness, in times to come, of the good opinion which such men had conceived of him, who knew the foundation

of

Mar: Ant: Flaminius, a great Scholar in Italy, writ to Galeacius, and congratulateth with him, for his holy and happy change.

of true justification, though they were yet possessed with other errors, as about the Sacraments, and of the Mass, &c. which alas, as yet they were not able to discern of, as after by the greater grace of God this *Galeacius* did. The Copy of the Letter is this,

CHAP. V.

Marcus Antonius Flaminius, a great Scholar in Italy, writeth to Galeacius, and congratulateth with him, for his holy and happy change.

To the Right Honourable, *Galeacius Carracciolus.*

Right Noble Lord, when I consider seriously these words of *Paul*; Brethren, you see your calling, that not many noble, not many wise, according to the flesh, not many mighty are called: but God hath chosen the foolish things of this world to confound the wise, and weak things to confound the mighty, and base things in the world, and things not accounted of, and things that are not, to bring to nought things that are. When, I say, I consider

of

of these words so often, I admire at that rare blessing of God, which he hath vouchsafed to you a Noble and mighty man: namely, that he should grace you with that true and incomparable Nobility, which is attained by true faith in Christ Jesus, and a holy life. As much greater as this blessing is, so much the more holy and sincere ought your life to be, and so much the more upright are you to walk with your God; lest that your thorns (that is, riches, pleasures, and honour,) should choke the seed of the Gospel, which is sown in you.

For this I am sure of, that God hath begun some great work in you, which he will finish to the glory of his own name, and will bring to pass, that as heretofore you had care so to live a Noble man amongst Noble men, that you might observe the decorum and maintain the dignity of Nobility: so hereafter that you may imploy your whole self in this, that you may defend and uphold the honour and dignity of the children of God, whose duty it is to aim at the perfection of their father with all endeavours; and in their life upon the earth to resemble that holy and heavenly life, which they shall lead in the world to come. Call to mind continually (my good Lord) in all your words and deeds, that

we

we are graced with this honour to be made the sons of God by Jesus Christ: for that meditation will by the help of the holy Ghost, work this care in us, that we never commit any thing unworthy of that holy name of Christ, by which we are called. And yet alas, such is our estate, as that if we do endeavour to please Christ, we are sure to displease men, and must be content to contemn the vain glory of the world, that we may enjoy heavenly and eternal glory with God; *for it is impossile (as Christ saith) for him to believe in God which seeks the honour and praise of men.* I mean of the men of this world, which as the Kingly Prophet saith, *are lighter and vainer than vanity it self.* And therefore their judgment is little worth, and less to be esteemed: but rather the judgment of God, who seeth not all our actions only, but even our most hidden thoughts and purposes. Which being so, were it not folly and madness to displease such a God, to please so fond a world? It were a shameful thing, if a Wife should indeavour to please other men, rather than her Husband. How much more then unworthy is it, if our souls should rather aim to please the vain world, than their most holy Spouse Christ Jesus? If the only Son of God was content not only to be reviled, yea and scourged and mocks, yea even the slanders of Gods enemies? Let us therefore arm our selves as it were with a holy pride, and (in a sort) scorn and laugh at their mocks; and putting upon us mercy and pity as the feeling members of Christ, let us bewail so great blindness in them, and let us intreat the Lord for them, to pull them out of that palpable darkness into his true and marvellous light, lest Satan bind them to himself in his everlasting prentiship; and so being his bond-slaves, and hired sworn servants of his black guard, do send them out to persecute Jesus Christ in his members. Which when they have done all they can, and all that the Devil their Master can teach them, though the Devil himself should burst with malice, and they for anger grind their teeth; yet shall it all tend to the magnifying of Gods glory, which they labour to obscure, and to the furtherance of their salvation, whom they so disdained: yea, to the increase of their glory in a better world, whom in this world they thought worthy of nothing but all disgrace: and surely (my most honorable Lord) he that is possessed with the certainty of this faith, will without doubt make

oper

open War with the corrupt affections of his own nature, and with all the world, yea even with the Devil himself; and will not doubt but in time even to overcome them all. Therefore let us humble our selves to our God & Father everlasting, that he would increase that faith in us, and bring forth in us those most blessed and sweet fruits of faith in our hearts & lives, which he useth to work in them whom he hath elected; that so our faith may appear not a fained, but a true faith; not a dead, but a living faith; not a humane but a divine work in us; that so it may be to us an infallible pledg of our salvation to come. Let us labour to shew our selves the legitimate and undoubted children of God in seeking above all things, that his most holy Name may be sanctified in our selves and others; and in imitating his admirable love and gentleness, which makes his Sun to shine on good and bad. Let us worship his heavenly Majesty in spirit and truth; and let us yield up the temple of our hearts to Christ Jesus, as an acceptable sacrifice unto him; yea, let us shew our selves members of the heavenly High Priest Christ Jesus, in sacrificing to God our bodies, and in crucifying the flesh with the affection, & lusts thereof; that sin being dead, God may create in us a spiritual life, whereby Christ Jesus may live

live in us. Let us dye to sin, and dye to our selves, and to the world, that we may live blessedly to God and Christ Jesus; yea let us acknowledg and shew by our lives, that we were once dead, but now are raised to the life of grace, by the power of Christ Jesus. Let our conversation be heavenly, though we live on the earth : let us begin that life here, which we hope to lead in heaven : let the Image of God shine bright in us : let us disgrace and wear out the old Image of sin and Satan, and labour to renew the Image of Christ Jesus, that all that see us may acknowledg Gods Image in us. Which holy Image of grace, as it is beautiful and glorious in all Gods Saints, so in you (my good Lord) it shall be so much more glorious, in as much as you go before others in Birth, Nobility, Honour, and high Place. O what a pleasant sight is it to all true Christian men, yea to the Angels; yea how acceptable to the Lord himself, to behold a man of your place and estate so far to forget the world and deny himself; so deeply to consider the frailty of his own nature, and the vanity of all temporal things, as to say with Christ, *I am a worm and no man*; and to cry out with *David, turn thy face to me, and have mercy upon me, for I am desolate and poor* : O happy and true rich man,
which

which hath attained to this spiritual and heavenly poverty, and can give a farewell to himself and the world, and all things that he hath for Christs sake; and can freely renounce and forsake carnal reason humane learning, company, and counsel of friends, wealth, Honours, Lordships, pleasures of all sorts, delight of the Court, high places, and preferments, dignity, and offices ; yea, favour of Princes ; yea, his own self! How welcome shall he be to Christ, which can deny all those for Christ sake ? Such a one may go for a Fool in the world, but he shall be of the Almighties counsel ; such a man knoweth that felicity consists not in any thing that this world can afford, and therefore in the midst of all his wealth and abundance, he crieth out to God as though he had nothing, even out of the feeling of his heart, *Give us this day our daily Bread.* Such a man preferreth the rebuke of Christ, before the honour of the world and the afflictions of Christs Religion, before the pleasures of the world : and because he despised all things in respect of Christ and his righteousness, and is possessed and grounded with Gods spirit, therefore he sings with true joy of heart with the kingly Prophet ; *The Lord is my Shepheard, therefore I can want nothing ; neither will I fear hun-*

ger or any outward thing; he feeds me in green pasture, and leads me forth beside the water of comfort. This man distrusts himself and all the creatures in the world, that he may trust and cleave only unto God; neither aimes he at any pleasure, any wisdom, any honour, any riches, any credit or estimation, but such as comes from God himself; and therefore professeth with the same Prophet: *I have none in heaven but thee alone, and none in the earth do I desire but thee, my flesh consumeth with longing after thee, and thou Lord art my heritage and portion for ever.* He that spake thus was a wealthy and mighty King, yet suffered he not the eyes of his mind to be blinded or dazled with the glittering glory of riches, pleasures, or honour, or ought else that a Kingdom could give; for he knew well that they all came of God, and were held under God, and must all be used to his glory, and that he that gave them hath far better things to give his children. And therefore that King and Prophet makes his heavenly proclamation before all his people; *Blessed art thou, O Lord God our Father, for ever and ever: thine O Lord is greatness, and power, and glory, and victory: all that is in heaven and earth is thine, thine is the Kingdom, Lord, and thou excellest as head over all: riches and honour*

nour come of thee, and thou art Lord of all: in thy hands is power, and strength, and honour, and dignity, and Kingdoms are in thy disposition: therefore we give thee thanks O God, and we extol thy great and glorious Name. But who am I, and what is my people, that we should promise such things to thee? For we are strangers before thee, and sojourners as all our fathers were; our days are like a shadow upon the earth, and here is no abiding.

See how *David* cannot content himself in abasing himself, and extolling the Lord; and in how many words his affections utter themselves. This was *Davids* meditation, and let this be your Looking-glass; in this Looking-glass look once a day, and pray daily, that God would still open your eyes to behold your own vileness, and his incomprehensible power and love to you, that with King *David* you may humble your self under the mighty hand of his Majesty, and acknowledg all power and glory to belong to God alone, that so you may be made partakers of those heavenly graces which God bestowed, not on the proud and lofty, but on the humble and meek. Remember that ordinance of the eternal God, that saith; *Let not the wise man glory in his wisdome, nor the strong man in his strength, nor the rich man in his riches, but let him that glo-*

rieth glory in this, in that he underſtandeth and knoweth me, that I am the Lerd which do mercy and juſtice on earth; for theſe things pleaſe me, ſaith the Lord. Therefore (my good Lord) if you liſt to boaſt, boaſt not as the world doth, that you are rich, or that you are of Noble birth, or that you are in favour with the Emperor and other Princes, or that you are heir apparent of a rich Marqueſdom, or that you have married ſo Noble a Woman; leave this kind of boaſting to them, who have their minds glewed to the World, and therefore have no better things to boaſt on; whoſe portion being here in this life, they can look for nothing in Heaven. But rather rejoyce you are entred into the kingdom of grace; glory in this, that the King of Kings hath had mercy on you, and hath drawn you out of the miſty darkneſs of errors, hath given you to feel his endleſs love and mercy in Chriſt, hath made you of the child of wrath, his own ſon; of a ſervant to ſin and the Devil, an heir of Heaven; and of a bondſlave to Hell, a Free Deniſon of the Heavenly Jeruſalem; and glory in this, that even Chriſt Jeſus himſelf is given you, and made your own, and with him all things elſe. So that as *Paul* ſaith, *all are yours, whether the world, or life, or death, things preſent or things to come, all are yours*

in

in and by Chrift, who is the only felicity of our fouls: and therefore whofoever have him, have with him all things elfe. This is the true glory and the found boafting of Chriftianity; for hereby is Gods mercy extolled, and mans pride trodden under foot, by which a man trufting too much to himfelf, rebelleth againft God. This glorious boafting makes us humble even in our higheft honours, modeft and meek in profperity, patient and quiet in adverfity; in troubles ftrong and couragious, gentle towards all men, joyfull in hope, fervent in prayer, full of the love of God, but empty of all love of our felves, or ought in the world; yea, it makes us Chrifts true Beadf-men, and his fworn fervants, and makes us yield up our felves wholly to imitate and follow Chrift, and to efteem all things elfe as frail and vain, *yea dung and drofs that we may win him.*

Right Honourable and my good Lord, you fee that I am fo willingly employed in this fervice of writing to your Honour, and in conferring with you of heavenly matters, that I have forgot my felf, or rather your Honour, in being fo tedious, which in the beginning I purpofed not. I am privy to my felf and of my own ignorance, and guilty of mine own infufficiency, as being fitter to be a Schollar than a Teacher; and to hear and learn my self, rather than to teach others; and therefore I crave pardon of your Honour. Farewell, The most reverend Embassador desireth in his heart he had occasion to testify indeed, that true good will which in his soul he bears you: In the mean time he salutes you, and so doth the illustrious Princess of *Piscaria* her Highness, and all other the Honourable Personages which are with me; all which rejoyce for this good work of God in you, and in all kindness do kiss your hands; and they do all earnestly intreat the Lord for you, that he that hath begun so great a work in you, would accomplish the same to the end; and the richer you are in temporal Goods, in Lands, and Lordships, that he would make you so much the more poor in spirit; that so your spiritual poverty, may do that which your wordly riches and honour cannot; namely, bring you at last to the eternal and never-fading riches of the world to come Amen. Farewell. From *Viturbium*.

Your Honours most humbly addicted, and most loving Brother in Christ,

M. Antonius Flaminius.

CHAP.

Of the many temptations the Devill used to pull him back, as by his father, his wife, and by noble men of his acquaintance.   p. 25

CHAP. VI.

Of the many temptations the Devil used to pull him back, as by his Father, his Wife, and by Noblemen of his acquaintance.

BY this and other holy means *Galeacius* was confirmed in the Doctrine of the Truth, and went forward constantly in the course of Gods calling, and the way of Godliness. But the more couragiously he went on, the more fiercely the Devil raged against him by his temptations, endeavouring thereby to hinder him in that happy course; yea and if it were possible to drive him back again; which course he commonly takes against those, who have propounded to themselves to tame the Rebellion of the flesh, and to relinquish the vanities of the world. And first of all, this zealous course of his in Religion procured him an infinite number of mocks, and made him subject to most vile slanders; yea made him incur the hatred of a great number, but especially did he herein displease and vex his Father, as one that was not only of a contrary Religion, but

but one who only intended the Honour of his House, and the advancing of his Posterity to all the honour that might be, which in respect of Religion *Galeacius* cared not for at all; and therefore he did often sharply chide him, and charged him with his Fatherly authority, to put away those melancholly conceits, (as he termed them.) No doubt but this was most grievous to him, who always was most submiss and obedient to his Father.

But another grief did more inwardly afflict him, which was in respect of his Wife *Victoria*; who though she was always a most kind and dutifull Wife, as also very wise, yet she would by no means yield to this motion and change of Religion; because she thought and feared it would breed infamy, and a reproach to her self and her house; and therefore was continually working on him by all means and devices she could; labouring to move him by tears and complaints, and by all kinds of intreaty that a Wife could use to her Husband; and withall sometimes urging him with such vain and fond reasons, as commonly women of that Religion are furnished withall. What a vexation this was, and what an impediment to his conversion, such may judg easily who are

cum-

cumbered with Husbands or Wives of a contrary Religion. And no little grief and temptation was it to him, besides all these, that the most part of the Noblemen in and about *Naples* (being either of his blood, or kindred, or his familiar friends) used continually to resort unto him, to follow their old and ordinary sports and pleasures. Alas how hard a thing was it to shake off all these on a sudden, and to take upon him a direct contrary course of life to that he had led with them afore; which he must needs do, if he would go on as he had begun? And further, it was no little vexation to his soul, to live in the Court, when his Office and Place called him thereunto; for there he might hear of any thing rather than of Religion, and not a word by any means of Gods Word, whereby to save his soul, but talk enough of common and wordly preferments and pleasures, and devising of means for the most cruel handling and dispatching out of the way all such as should depart from the Romish Faith. Any Christian heart may easily conceive how deeply those temptations and hindrances vexed his righteous soul in this his course towards God; in so much as a thousand to one they had

had turned him back again; and doubtlef they had done so indeed, had not God affifted him with fpecial grace.

CHAP. VII.

How he efcaped the fnares of the Arians, Anabaptifts, *and after of the* Waldefians; *and of his refolution to leave his Country, Honours and Livings, to enjoy the benefit of Gods Religion.*

But above all thefe, Satan had one affault ftrongeft of all, whereby he attempted to feduce him from the true and fincere Religion of God. About that time the Realm of *Naples* was fore peftered with *Arians*, and *Anabaptifts*, who daily broched their herefies amongft the common people, colouring them over with glorious fhews. Thefe fellows perceiving *Galeacius* not fully fetled as yet in Religion, nor yet fufficiently grounded in the Scripture, tryed all means they could to entangle him in their errors and blafphemous fancies; wherein the mighty work of God was admirable towards him, for he being a Youth, a Gentleman, but a mean Scholar, and little

little studied, and but lately entred into the School of Christian Religion, who would have thought that ever he could have resisted and escaped the snares of those Hereticks, many of them being great and grounded Scholars, and throughly studied in the Scripture? Notwithstanding, by the sincere simplicity and plainness of Gods truth, and the inspiration of the Holy Ghost, he not only descried the fondness of their heresies, but even untied the knots, and brake their nets and delivered himself, and mightily confuted them; yea such was the working of God, as being sometime in their meetings, he was strongly confirmed in the Doctrine of the Truth by seeing and hearing them. Thus by God's mercy he escaped, and was conqueror in this fight.

But the Devil had not so done with him, for another and more dangerous battel presently followed. The *Waldesians* of whom we spake before, were at that time in *Naples* in good number. With them did *Galeacius* daily converse, their courses of life and study being not far unlike. These Disciples of *Waldesius* knew as yet no more in Religion but the point of Justification, and misliked and eschewed some abuses in Popery, and nevertheless still frequented Popish Churches,
heard

heard Masses, and were present ordi[nary at their]
vile Idolatries. *Galeacius* for a time [convers-]
sed with these men, and followed the[ir courses]
which course doubtless would have [undone]
him, as did a great sort of them; w[ho after-]
wards being taken and committed [for the]
Truth, were easily brought to reca[nt their]
Religion, because they wanted the c[learness of]
the most excellent points, nor were [suffi-]
ciently setled; and yet afterwards [repenting]
not daring to forsake their hold in J[ustifica-]
tion, and therefore coming to it aga[in, were]
taken as relapsers and backsliders, an[d put to]
extream torments, and cruel death. In [which]
danger had *Galeacius* been, but that t[he good]
providence of God otherwise dispos[ed and]
better provided for him; for his O[ffice and]
Place that he bare in the Emperor['s Court]
called him into *Germany*, and so wi[thdrew]
him from his Companions the *Wa*[*ldesians*;]
for the Lord had a greater work t[o work]
in him than the *Waldesians* were able [to teach]
him; for there in *Germany* he learne[d (which]
he never knew afore) that the kn[owledge]
of the truth of Justification was not s[ufficient]
for salvation; whilest in the mean [time a]
man wittingly defiled himself with I[dolatry,]
which the Scripture calls spiritual [Whore-]
dom; and of no man did he rea[d or hear]

found and comfortable instruction than of *Peter Martyr*, of whom we spake afore, whom God hath lately called out of *Italy* and confirmed him in the truth. This *Martyr* instructed *Galeacius* soundly in the way of truth, and made it plain, by private conferences as well as publick; for he was then publick Professor of Divinity at *Strasborough* in *Germany*. *Galeacius* furnished with those instructions, returned to *Naples*, and presently resorting to his companions the *Waldesians*, amongst other points conferred with them about the eschewing of Idolatry, and delivered his judgment therein. But they not induring scarce to hear it, presently forsook him; for they would by no means entertain that Doctrine, which they knew was sure to bring upon them afflictions, persecutions, loss of Goods and Honours, or else would cause them to forsake Country, House, and Land, Wife, and Child, and so every way threatned a miserable estate to the Professor thereof. Now this their forsaking of him, and telling him of the danger of this Profession, was another strong temptation to keep him wrapped in their Idolatry, and to make him content himself with their imperfect and pieced Religion. But GOD, who had in his eternal election predistinated him, that

he

he should be a singular example of constancy to the edification of many, and the confusion and condemnation of luke-warm professors, gave him that excellent resolution, and that heavenly courage, as he escaped at last conqueror over all those temptations and assaults of Satan; and nothing could suffice or content him but the pure Religion, and also the profession of it; and therefore seeing no hope of reformation in *Naples*, nor any hope to have the *Waldesians* joyn with him, and seeing plainly that he could not serve God in the Country, he resolved undoubtedly that he would forsake the Country, and seek for Christ and his Religion wheresoever he might find them; and that he would rather forsake Father, Wife, Children, Goods and Lands, Offices and Preferments to win Christ, than to enjoy them all and want Christ Jesus.

CHAP. VIII.

Of the grievous combats betwixt the flesh and the spirit, when he resolved of his departure.

Now here by the way it may not be omitted, what kind of cogitations he hath often

often said came into his mind, as he was deliberating about this great matter. For first of all, as often as he looked on his father, which he did almost every hour, who dearly loved him, and whom again he respected in all duty and reverence: so often doubtless he was stricken at the heart with unspeakable grief to think of his departure, his mind no doubt often thinking thus: What, and must I needs forsake my dear and loving father, and cannot I else have God my Father? O miserable and unhappy father of my body, which must stand in comparison with the Father of my soul! And must I needs fail in duty to him, if I perform my duty to God? O miserable old man! for what deeper wound can pierce him, than thus to be deprived of the only staff and comfort of his age? Alas, shall I thus leave him in such a Sea of troubles; and shall I be the only means to strike into his heart the deepest wound of grief that yet ever pierced him in all his life? This my departure is sure to make my self the Obloquie of the World: yea, to breed reproach and shame to the Marquess my Father, and to my whole Stock and Kindred.

How is it possible that the good old man can overcom or indure so great a greif, but rather he must needs be swallowed up of it, and so with

with wo and misery end his life; Shall I then be the cause of death to my father, who would, if need had been, redeemed my life with his own death? alas! what a misery is this like to be either to me, or him, or us both? yet must I care less for bringing his gray head with sorrow unto the grave, than for casting my own poor Soul with horror into Hell. And no less inwardly was he grieved in respect of his noble Wife *Victoria* : for having no hope that she would renounce Popery, and go with him, therefore he durst not make known unto her the purpose of his departure; but rather resolved for Christ sake to leave her and all, and to follow Christ. She was now as he was himself in the prime of Youth, a Lady of great birth, fair, wise, and modest; but her love and loyalty to her Husband surpassed all. How was it possible patiently to leave such a Wife, so that his perplexed mind discoursed on this fashion when he lookt on her? And shall I so, yea so suddenly and so unkindly leave and forsake my Wife, my most deer and loving Wife, the only joy of my heart in this world, my companion and partner in all my grief and labour: the augmenter of my joy, the lessener of my wo? And shall I leave her, not for a time (as heretofore I did, when the Emperors service
called

called me from her) but for ever, never again
to enjoy her, yea, it may be never to see her?
And shall I deprive my self of her, and thereby deprive my self of all others also, and of
all the conjugal life and married estate? And
shall I so leave her desolate and alone in that
estate and age whereof she is? Alas poor
Lady, what shall she do? what shall become
of her, and of her poor little ones, when I
am gon? How many dolefull days without comfort, many waking nights without
sleep, shall she pass over? What will she
do but weep and wail, and pine away with
grief? And as he cast these things in his
mind, he thought he even saw his Wife,
how she took on with her self, sighing, and
sobbing, and weeping; yea howling and crying, and running after him with these pitifull
out-cries: Ah my dear Lord, and sweet Husband whither will you go? and will you leave
me miserable Woman, comfortless and suc-
courless? What shall become of me, when
you are gon? What can honours, pomps,
riches, gold, silver, jewels, friends, company,
all delights and pleasures in the earth, what
can they all do to my comfort when I want
you? And what joy can I have in my children without you, but rather my grief to be
doubled to look on them? And how can I or

the world be perswaded that you care for them, and for my self? Is this the love that thou so often boasted of? Ah! miserable love which had this issue! either never didst thou love me, else never had true love so strange an end as this of yours hath. And yet, which is worse than all this, you never shewed me the cause of this your strange departure: had I known cause, it would never have grieved me half so much: But now that the cause is not known, what will the world judge, but the fault is in me? at least, if they cannot condemn me for it; yet how reproachfull will it be to me, when every base Companion dare lay it in my dish, and point at me with their fingers when I go by, and say, This is that fond Woman, who married him with whom she could not live, and whom her Husband disdained to live withall? This is that simple fool, who is desolate having a Husband, and a Widow, her Husband yet being alive. Either shall I be counted wicked, which have caused thee to leave me, or foolish, miserable, and unhappy, who chose so fondly, as to take him whom I could not be sure of when I had him. In a word, I shall be deprived of thee: yea of all possibility of having any other, and so having a Husband, and of a Noble Family, I shall

live

live in all misery, altogether without a Husband. These two cogitations of his Father and his Wife greatly tormented him, and the more because he laboured to keep close this fire, which burned and boiled in his heart: namely, to conceal his departure, left by being known, it might be hindred, which he would not for a World.

Yet there was a third and special care that pinced him, and that was for his Children, which were six in all; goodly and towardly children, and worthy of so noble Parents: the more grief was it, in that they were so young, as that they could not yet conceive what it was to want a Father; the eldest was scarce fifteen, and the youngest scace four years old: he loved them with most tender and fatherly affection, and was again loved and honoured of them. It is wonderful to think, how when his Wife the Lady did give into his armes his youngest child to play withall (as oftentimes Wives use to do) how it were possible for him and what adoe he had with himself to contain from flouds of tears; especially because his eyes seeing them, and his heart taking delight and pleasure in them, his mind could not but discourse on this manner: And shall I within these few days utterly forsake these sweet

sweet babes, and leave them to the wide and wicked world, as though they had never been my children, nor I their father? Yea happy had I been, if I had either never had them, or having them might enjoy them: To be a father of no children, and yet to have children, that is a misery. And you poor Orphans, what shall become of you when I am gon? your hap is heard, even to be fatherless, your father yet living; and what can your great birth now help you? for by my departure you shall lose all your living and wealth, and all your dignity whatsoever, which otherwise you had been sure of: nay, my departure shall not only deprive you of all this, but lay you open to all infamy, reproach, and slander, and bring upon you all kind of misery. And thus, then shall the time be cursed that ever they had me to their father. And what can your wofull mother do when she looketh on you, but weep and wring her hands, her grief still increasing as she looks upon you? Yet thus must I leave you all confounded together in heaps of griefs, weeping and wailing one with another, and I in the mean time weeping and wailing for you all. Many other griefs, temptations and hindrances assaulted him, though they were not so weighty as these formerly named, yet which

which might have been able to have hindred any mans departure, being in his cafe; as to leave the company of fo many gallant Noblemen and Gentlemen, his kindred and acquaintance; to lofe fo honourable an Office, and place he bare in the Emperors Court; to leave for ever his native Soil, the delicate *Italy*; to deprive himfelf and his pofterity of the noble Title and rich living of a Marquefdom; to undertake a moft long and tedious journey; to caft himfelf into exile, poverty, fhame, and many other miferies without hope of recovery for ever; to change his former pleafant life into all hardnefs, and give a farewell to all the delicacies of *Italy*, wherein he was brought up, to leave that goodly Garden of his Father the Marqueffes, which once fhould be his own; the goodlieft Garden almoft in all *Italy*, or all Chriftendom, which was furnifhed with plants of all forts, and thefe not only of all that grow in *Italy*, but even fuch as were to be got out of all other Countries: This Garden and Orchard was fo exquifite both this way, and in divers other forts of Elegancies, that a great number of men of all qualities reforted daily out of all Countries to fee it. But this and all other the pleafures and delicacies of this prefent life could do nothing with him to remove him

D 4   from

from his purpose; but he renounced them all, and resolved to leave them all, to follow Christ: so strong and admirable was the constancy of this noble Gentleman.

CHAP. IX.

How after all the temptations which flesh and blood had in his way to hinder his departure, he consulted with the Lord, and from him received grace to overcome them all.

BUT it may be asked, Whereupon was grounded so great unmoveableness of this purpose, or whence came it? If we ask the world and common judgment, they will answer, that doubtless melancholick humors prevailing in him, spoiled the man of his judgment and natural affections, and impaired common sense and reason; and thence proceeded this obstinate and desperate purpose, as the world judgeth of it. But if a man lift up his eyes higher, and behold the matter more seriously, he might have manifestly seen that it came to pass by the mercifull blessing and strong Hand of God, who from all eternity had predestinated him, that

he

he should stand so unmoveable against all temptations, and continue in one tenour steady and stedfast, until he had made void all the attempts of Satan and removed all the stumbling blocks which his flesh and blood, and carnal reason could cast in the way; for the which purpose the Spirit of God enabled him to reason with himself on this sort; Thou Lord art he who drew and deliveredst me out of the thick and misty darkness of ignorance, and hast enlightned my mind with the light of thy holy Spirit, and with the heavenly knowledg of thy Truth: Thou hast made known to me the way of Salvation, and hast ransomed me, to thy self by the blood of thy Son. Now therefore good Lord and holy Father, I am wholly thine, and consecrated to thy glory; and as I am thine, I will follow thee and obey thee, and walk in the way of thy Will whither soever thou shalt call me. Not my Father, nor my Wife, nor my Children, nor my Honours, nor my Lands, nor my Riches, nor all my Delicacies and Pleasures shall hold or hinder me one hour from following thee. I deny my self, O Lord, and I deny this whole World for thee and thy sake; O Lord, thou knowest me, and the readiness of my mind to wait upon thee, and how that my heart is inflamed with the fire of of thy love: Yet thou seest again how many enemies compass me, how many hindrances lie in my way, and how many temptations and impediments lie upon me, so that I am scarce able to move or lift up my head unto thee: O Lord, I am now in the depths of those troubles, out of which the holy Prophet *David* once cried to thee, as I do now; *O Lord, have mercy on me, and deliver my soul.* And although Satan and my own flesh do affright me in this my purpose, whilst they set before mine eyes, the cross, the infamy, and the poverty, and so many miseries, which I am like in this my new profession to undergo: notwithstanding, O Lord, I lift up my self in the contemplation and beholding of thy infinite Majesty, and therein I see and confess, that the cross and affliction is blessed and glorious, which makes me like, and conformable to Christ my head; and that infamy to be honourable, which sets me in the way to true honour; and that poverty to be desired, which depriving a man of some temporal goods, will reward him with an heavenly inheritance, than which, there is nothing more precious, I mean, O Lord, with thine own Self, and thy Glory: O everlasting God, and that by thy only Son Jesus Christ: that so enjoying thy glorious Presence, may live

live for ever with thee in that heavenly Society : O blessed and happy these miseries that pull me out of the worlds vanities, and sink of sin, that I may be made heir of an everlasting Glory. Welcome therefore the Cross of Christ, I will take it up, O Lord, and will follow thee.

With these and such like holy meditations, and other holy means, he overcame at last the attempts of Satan, all his own natural and carnal affections; yea, and the world it self, and verified that in himself which *Paul* affirmeth of Gods true Elect, that *they that are Chrifts, have crucified the flesh with the affections and lusts* : that is, have crucified their Souls for Christ, who crucified himself for them. O Satan, Gods Enemy and his Childrens, how vain were all thy attempts, and how light all thy assaults ? in vain doest thou set upon those for whom Christ vouchsafed to dye, and suffer on the Cross : upon which Cross he so brake thy head and thy power, and so trampled over thee, that now thou shalt not be able to touch the least hair of the head of any of those for whom he died. And as for *Galeacius*, he had builded his house on the Rock, and founded it so sure; that no wind, no rain, nay no floods of griefs, nor tempests of troubles, nor whirl-wind of tempta-

temptations could once remove him : and so he continued resolute as a Christian Souldier and Conqueror ; fully minded to leave his Countrey at the next opetunity he could take : his mind I cannot tell whether more ravished with joy one way, or more perplexed with grief another way : but betwixt joy and grief he still continued his purpose, until at last his spiritual joy overcoming his natural and carnal grief, he fully concluded, that in despight of the Devil and all impediments in the World, he will surely go.

CHAP. VII.

How he performed his heroical resolution, leaving all for Christ, and going to Geneva.

WHereupon, making known his mind but to a few, and those his most familiar Friends, and of whom he hoped well for Religion ; he wrought upon them so far, as that they promised and vowed they would accompany him in his voluntary and Christian banishment, that so they might enjoy the true liberty and peace of
con-

conscience in the true Church of God. But how deep and unsearchable the judgments of God are, the event afterward shewed: for divers of them (though not all) who for a time seemed to be indued and lead with a most earnest zeal of Gods glory in this action; when they came to the borders of *Italy*, and considered what they forsook, and to what they now took temselves: first began to look back again to *Italy*; afterwards went back again indeed, and so turned again to the vomit of their pleasures.

But this ingratitude to the Lord for so great a favour offered them, the Lord pursued with a just revenge: for purposing to serve God in their pleasures, and in the midst of Popery, they were after taken by the *Spanish* Inquisition; and so publickly recanting and abjuring Christian Religion, they were afterward subject to all misery and infamy, neither trusted nor loved of the one side nor the other. This fearfull disfertion and backsliding of theirs, doubtless was most grievous to *Galeacius*: and verily the Devil hoped hereby yet once again to have diverted him from his intended course, in making him be forsaken of those, by whose Company and Society he hoped to have been greatly comforted in this discomfortable Voyage. But notwithstanding

ding all this, *Galeacius* continued resolute in his purpose, and at last finding opportunity, attempted his departure, and made fit for it; yet made no shew of any such matter; but rather coloured and concealed his intent, lest the authority of his father might any way hinder his so godly purpose: and so gathering together four thousand marks of his mothers goods which she had left him; On the one and twentieth of *March*, 1551, in the year of his age the four and thirtieth, he departed from *Naples* in manner as he was wont to do afore, making it known that he purposed to go into *Germany* to the Emperor; who at that time held his Court at *Auspurge*, and thither indeed he went accordinly, and stayed serving in his place and Office, till the six and twentieth of *May* in the same year: Upon which day leaving the Court and the Emperors Service, and his Honourable Office which there he bare; and taking his last and everlasting farewell at the Court, and all worldly delights, (and yet departing in ordinary sort as before, and in purpose to go into the *Low-Countries*, as some thought) he took his journey straight toward *Geneva*, and thither came by Gods good hand the eighth of *June*, and there rested his weary, and reposed his much more wearied ed conscience, with a full joyful heart: yea with the greatest joy that ever came to him in all his life, but only at the time of his conversion.

CHAP. XI.

Of his arival at Geneva, *and his entertainment there: and especially his acquaintance and friendship with* Calvin.

IN the City of *Geneva* (though there was a Church of *Italians*, who likewise were come thither for the Gospel) yet he found not one whom he knew, save one *Lactantius Rangonius*, a Noble man of *Siena* in *Italy*; this Gentleman had been one of his familiar acquaintance when they were at home, and now was Preacher of Gods Word to the Church and Congregation of the *Italians*, who were then at *Geneva*. Now when he saw that the mercy of God had granted him to arrive at this quiet and happy Haven, where he might with liberty of conscience serve God, free from the corruptions of the world; and the abominable Superstitions and Idolatry of Antichrist;

tichrist; presently he joyned himself to the instruction of Master *John Calvin*, the chief Minister and Preacher of that Church. *Calvin* being a man of deep insight and exquisite judgment, perceiving him to be a man of good knowledg and experience, of a moderate and quiet spirit, of an innocent and upright Life, and indued with true and sincere godliness; did therefore most kindly and lovingly entertain him into his fellowship: for the good man of God in his Wisdom foresaw that such a man as this, would doubtless become a special instrument of Gods glory, and means of the confirmation of many (but especially of *Italians*) in the knowledg and love of Religion: This holy love and Christian friendship thus began, was so strongly grounded betwixt this Noble Marquess and renowned *Calvin*, that it continued till the year 1564, which was the last year of *Calvins* pilgrimage on the earth, and the entrance into his heavenly rest. The Church and people of *Geneva* can testifie of their truth & constant friendship: but it needs not; for there is extant at this day a special testimony thereof, even from *Calvin* himself in this Preface of his; wherein he dedicates to *Galeacius*, his Commentary upon the first Epistle to the *Corinths*; which I thought good

Calvine sends an Epistle to Galeacius congratulating his holy and happy conversion. p. 4

good here to set down word by word, that thereby it may appear how greatly *Calvin* esteemed of him.

CHAP. XII.

Calvins *Epistle to* Galeacius, *congratulating his holy and happy conversion.*

To the Noble Gentleman, and as well Honorable for his excellent vertues, as for his high descent and lineage, Galeacius Caracciolus, *the only son and heir apparent to the Marquess of* Vicum : John Calvin *sendeth greeting in our Lord.*

I Wish that when I first put out this Commentary, I had either not known at all, or at least more throughly known that man, whose Name I am now constrained to blot out of this my Epistle : Yet I fear not at all, lest he should either upbraid me with inconstancy, or complain of injury offered him, in taking that from him which afore I bestowed on him; because it was his own seeking.

seeking both to estrange himself from me, and from all society with our Church, wherefore he may thank himself, and take the blame on his own neck; for, for my own part I am unwillingly drawn thus far to change my accustomed manner, as to race out any mans Name out of my writing. And I bewaile that the man hath thrown himself down from that seat of fame wherein I have placed him; namely, in the forefront of my Book; where my desire was he should have stood, thereby to have been made famous to the World, But the fault is not in me, for as then I held him worthy, so since then he hath made himself unworthy; and therefore let him be as he is, and lie for me buried in oblivion; and so for the good-will I once bear to him, I spare to speak any more of him. And as for you (Right Honourable Sir) I might seek excuse why I put you now in his room, but that I am so sufficiently perswaded of your great good will and true love to me, the truth whereof can be testified by so many witnesses in our Church. And that I make one wish more from my heart, that I had known you as well ten years ago, for then I should have had no cause to have altered the Dedication of my Book, as now I do.

And

And as for the publick estate of the Church, it is well that it shall not only lose nothing by forgetting that man, whose Name I now blot out, but by yours coming into his stead, shall receive a far greater gain, and a sufficient recompence. For though I know you desire not the publick applause of the world, but rest contented in the testimony of Gods spirit in your conscience: (neither is it my purpose to publish your praises to the world) notwithstanding, I think it my duty to make known to the Reader some things concerning you, and whereof my self and this Church and City are daily eye-witnesses; and yet not so mnch for your praise, as for the benefit and instruction of the Readers. And this is it that I would all men should know and make use of; that a Gentleman, a Lord, so well and highly born, flourishing in wealth and honour, blessed with a noble, and virtuous, and loving Wife, and many goodly Children, living in all peace and quietness at home and abroad, wanting nothing that Nature could desire, and every way blessed of God for all things of this life, should willingly and of his own accord leave all those, and forsake his Country, a rich, and fruitful, and pleasant soil; so goodly a patrimony and inheritance, so stately a house,

seated

seated so commodiously and so pleasantly to cast off all domestical delight and joy which he might have had in so good a Father, Wife, Children, Kindred, affinity and acquaintance, all that for this only, that he might come and serve Christ Jesus in the hard and unpleasant warrfare of Christianity; and should deprive himself of so many alluring delights of Nature, and to content himself with that slender measure of all things, which the distressed state of our Church is able to afford; and from all the superfluities of a Courtly and Lordly life, here amongst us to betake himself to an easy rare and frugal kind of life, even as though he were no better than one of us; and yet though I so recite all this to others, so I let it not pass without use to my self. For if I do set out your vertues in this my Epistle, as on the top of a Tower for all men to see them, that so they may conform themselves to the imitation of them, it should be shame for my self not to be much nearly and inwardly touched with a love of them, who am continually an eye-witness of them, and daily behold them, not in an Epistle, but in the clear glass of your own life; and therefore, because that I find in experience, how much your example pre-
vails

vails in me for the strengthening of my faith, and the increase of godliness in me; (yea, and all other holy men who dwell in the City, do acknowledg as well as I, that this your example hath been greatly to their edification in all grace:) I thought it therefore a necessary duty to impart this rare example of yours to the world, that so the profit and benefit of us might enlarge it self, and spread out of this City into all the Churches of God; for otherwise it were a needless labour to make known to the furthest parts of Christendom, the vertues of such a man, whose nature and disposition is so out of love with pride, and so far removed from all ostentation. Now if it shall please God that many others (who dwelling far off, have not hitherto heard of you) shall by the strangeness of this your example address themselves to the imitation of it, and leave their pleasant nests, whereto the world hath setled them so fast, I shall think my self bountifully rewarded for these my pains; for out of question it should be common and usual amongst Christians, not only to leave Livings, and Lordships, and Castles, and Towns, and Offices, and promotions, when the case so stands, that a man may not enjoy both
Christ

Christ and them; but even willingly and chearfully to despise and shake off whatsoever under the Sun (though it be never so dear and precious, so pleasant and comfortable) in respect and comparison of Christ. But such is the slowness and sluggishness of the most of us, that we do but coldly and formally profess the Gospel; but not one of a hundred, if he have but some little Land, or piece of a Lordship, that will forsake and despise it for the Gospels sake; yea not one of many, but very hardly is drawn to renounce even the least gain or pleasure, to follow Christ without it; so far are they from denying themselves, and laying down their lives for the defence of it. I wish these men would look at you, and observe what it is you have forsaken for love of Christ, and especially I wish that all men who have taken upon them already the profession of Religion, would labour to resemble you in the denial of themselves, (which indeed is the chief of all heavenly vertues;) for you can very sufficiently testify with me, as I can with you, how little joy we take in these mens companies, whose lives make it manifest, that though they have left their Countreys, yet they have brought hither with them the
same

same affections, difpositions which they had at home; which if they had alfo renounced, as well as they did their Countries, then had they indeed been true deniers of themfelves, and been partakers with you of that true praife, wherein alas, you have but few co-partners. But becaufe I had rather the Reader fhould gather the truth and ftrangenefs of this our example, than I fhould go about in words to exprefs it; I will therefore fpare further fpeech, and turn my felf to God in prayer, defiring of his mercy, that as he hath indued you hitherto with an heroical courage and fpiritual boldnefs, fo he would furnifh you with an invincible conftancy to endure to the end: for I am not ignorant how ftrangely the Lord hath exercifed you heretofore, and what dangerous pikes you have paffed ere you came to this; by which former experience your fpiritual wifdom is able to conclude, that a hard and toilfome warfare doth ftill remain and wait for you; and what need there is to have the hand of God from Heaven raught out to affift us, you have fo fufficiently learned in your former conflicts, as I am fure you will joyn with me in Prayer, for the gift of perfeverance to us both: and for my part I will not ceafe to befeech Jefus Chrift our King and God, (to whom all power was given of his Father, and in whom are kept all the treasures of spiritual blessings) that he would still preserve you safe in soul and body, and arm you against all temptations to come, and that still he wou'd proceed to triumph in you over the Devil, and all his vile and wicked faction, to the magnifying of his own glory, and the inlarging of his Kingdom in your self, and others of his children. *9 Cal. Febr.* 1556. at *Geneva.*

Your Honours most assured
in the Lord

JOHN CALVIN.

CHAP. XII.

News of his departure to Geneva *came to* Naples *and the Emperors Court; and how the old Marquess his Father and other his friends were affected with the News.*

ANd thus (to return again to our story) *Galeacius* setled himself down at *Geneva*, as at a joyful resting place. But when the news of so sudden and strange a departure, and so wilful an exile, came to *Naples*, and were made known in the Emperors Court, it would scarce be believed or thought, how strangely it affected and moved all that heard it. All men wondered at it, and the most could not be perswaded it was so; but when it was certainly known, and out of doubt, it was strange to see how every man gave his verdict of the matter; some one way, some another, as the course of men in such cases is; but above all, it so abashed and astonished his own friends and family, that nothing was heard or seen amongst them but crys and lamentations,

most

most bitter tears, and pittiful complaints. And surely to have beholden the state of that Family, how miserable it seemed at that time to be distressed, a man would have thought it even a lively pattern and picture of all wo and misery. But none was more inwardly pinched than the Marquess his Father, whose age and experience being great, seemed to assure him of nothing to follow hereupon but infamy and reproach, yea the utter undoing and subversion of his whole estate and family; notwithstanding, passing over that fit of sorrow as soon and as easily as he could, the wretched and careful old man began to bethink himself by what means he might prevent so miserable a ruine and fall, which seemed to hang over him and his. One thing amongst other came into his mind, which also has once caused many grievous temptations to *Galeacious*, and had much troubled his mind afore his departure. It was this.

CHAP.

CHAP. XIV.

The first means used by his Father, the old Marquess to recall him home again; he sent a Kinsman of his, whom he knew his son dearly loved, to perswade him to return, but he could not prevail.

G*Aleacius* had a Cousen german, whom always he esteemed and loved as his brother; this Gentleman so tenderly loved of *Galeacius*, did the Marquess send to *Geneva* to his son, with Commission and Letters full of authority, full of protestations, full of pittiful complaints, full of cryings, and intreatings that he would come home again, and thereby chear up his old Father, and make happy again his unhappy Wife, be a comfort to his distressed Children, a rejoycing to his Kinsfolks, and to the whole City of *Naples*, and save his whole house and posterity from that extreme ruine, which otherwise it would be sure to fall into. Thus this Gentleman was dispatched away
and

and hasted to *Geneva*, with great hope, for their antient and faithful love to have prevailed with *Galeacius*; whereby the way we are to remember, that *Galeacius* did always so love him, that the Gentleman was not so sorrowful for his departure, but *Galeacius* was much more sorrowful that he could not win him to have gon with him in his holy Pilgrimage for Religions sake; but he so much feared to have been hindred himself, that he durst not deal with this Gentleman his dearest Cosen, no nor with his Wife, to perswade them to have gon with him. The Gentleman coming to *Geneva*, enquired after *Galeacius*: At that time *Galeacius* dwelt in an ordinary and mean house, which he had taken to his own use, having no more attendance but only two servants. The Gentleman at last found him out, and presented himself into his sight? It had been a pittiful spectacle to have seen the meeting of those two Gentlemen; their first meeting and imbracings were nothing at all but sighs and sobs, and tears, and in utterable signs of grief; such unspeakable sorrow did their natural affections breed in them, that for divers hours they could not speak a word one to another; but at last the Gentleman, burning

in

in desire to enjoy again his dearest *Galeacius*, burst forth into speaches, and mixing tears and sobs with every word, delivered his Letters till he could come to more liberty of speach; and at last having obtained of his affections leave to speak, he added to his Letters, exhortations, strong perswasions, earnest intreaties, and withall plenty of tears, that he would have respect to the overthrow of his House, the grief of his old Father, the desparate estate of his Wife and Children, the continual complaints made by all his friends and kinsfolks; all which notwithstanding were not so past cure, but that yet they might be remedied by his return again This was the substance of his message. *Galeacius* taking not long time to advise himself in this, which the world would think so weighty a case, addressed him immediately this answer in brief: That he perceived very well all to be true that he said; but as for his departure, it was not done rashly, nor upon any fond conceit, but upon mature deliberation; that the Lord was the author of the action, that Gods grace was the cause moving him, and the means whereby he brought it to pass; which grace of God, he said, had opened his eyes, and enlightned his mind with the

the knowledg of the truth, and made him see and discern the cosenages, and superstitions, and Idolatry of Popery; which by an impious and sacrilegious distribution divideth the glory of God (which is imcommunicable) and imparteth the same with fained and filthy Idols: he likewise told him, that he well foresaw all the infamies and miseries which would ensue upon this his conversion; and all danger and dammage which thereby his House and Children were likely to incur. But he said, that seeing one of these must needs be chosen, either to stay at home with a conscience burdened with a heavy heap of errors and superstitions, piled together by the sleight of Satans art, and every moment to sin against the Majesty of God so many thousand ways; or else to leave his house, his goods his Family, his Country, yea the World, and all the glory of it, and thereby purchase liberty of conscience to serve the Lord according to his Word; that therefore he resolved, of the two evils to chuse the less, and of the goods to chuse the greater; and rather to shut his eyes at all these, than the sight of them should hinder him from yeilding to the call and voice of his Saviour Christ; who saith, *That a man is not worthy*

worthy to be his disciple, who leaveth not father and mother, and children, and brethren, and sisters; yea, and his own life in comparison of him. And this he said was the cause, why he did forsake Parents, and Wife, and Children, and all his Friends, and had renounced all his wealth and dignities, because he could not enjoy both Christ and them. And as for them all, he was sorry that either they would not come to him, or that he might not more safely live with them thereby to comfort them. But as for himself, he said he had riches, and honour, and joy enough; yea, all sufficient happiness, as long as (with these two Servants and his little Cottage) he might live in the true Church of God, and might purely serve him, and might enjoy Gods Word and Sacraments, not being mixed and defiled with the superstitious devices of mans brain; and as long as he might live in the company of godly men,, and have time and liberty to meditate by himself, and confer with them of the great blessings which in his conversion his good God had vouchsafed to him; that so he might with true contentation and perfect peace of conscience, aim and aspire at that immortal glory which Christ hath prepared for all his children:

children: yea he concluded, that his want was abundance, his poverty pleasant, and his mean estate honourable in his eyes, as long as he endured them for these conditions.

This his answer was as hardly entertained of his Kinsman, as it was unlooked for afore it came; but seeing he could not reply with any reason, nor answer him with any shew of argument; and perceived it hard, or rather impossible to remove the man one jot from his resolution: for that he had grounded it, not on any reason or will of man, but upon the holy Word of God, and his powerful and unresistable calling; therefore with a sorrowful heart he held his tongue, bitterly complaining within himself of his so hard hap, and uncomfortable success; and so resolved to return home again, heartily wishing that he had never taken that journey in hand; and so at last he went indeed and took his leave of his beloved *Galeacius*, but not without plenty of tears on both sides, with many a woful cry and pittiful farewell. And no marvel, for besides nearness of blood, their likeness in manners and daily conversation together had linked them in a sure bond of friendship; but there wanted

in

in one of them the sureſt link in that chain, that is, Religion, aud so it could not hold: and therefore the world pulling the other of them from the World, so theſe two friends left each other, being in fear never to see one the other again.

CHAP. XV.

Of his Coſens return to Naples *without ſucceſs, and how* Galeacius *was ploclaimed Traitor for his departure.*

ANd thus at laſt he came home to *Naples* with heavy chear. Whoſe approach being heard of, their was running on all ſides to hear good news: but when he had delivered his meſſage; alas! how all their ſorrow was redoubled upon them; and how his father, wife, children, and all his friends were overwhelmed with grief: and the rather, becauſe as at the ſame time an Edict was publiſhed, wherein *Galeacius* was proclaimed guilty of high Treaſon: and therefore all his goods coming to him by his mother, were confiſcate, and him-

himself, and all his posterity utterly cut off, and excluded from all right of succession in his fathers Marquesdom ; which thing (above all other) grievously affected the old Marquess, and grieved the good old man at the very heart ; the advancing and honouring of his posterity being the only thing he aimed at all his life. Whereupon he bethought himself as old as he was, to make a journey to *Cæsar* the Emperor, and thereby if it were possible to prevent this mischief : purposing to make but this suit to his Majesty, That his sons departure for the *Roman* Church, might not prejudice nor hinder the succession and honour of his Children and posterity, but that he himself might only bear the punishment of his own fault.

CHAP.

CHAP. XVI.

Of the second means used to recall him: his father sent for him to come and meet him at Verona; but all he could do by himself or others whom he set on prevailed nothing at all.

And whilst he was resolving of this purpose, he bethought him of another remedy and means, whereby he hoped to remove his sons mind from his purpose, and withdraw him from the company of those Hereticks of *Geneva*, as he and the world accounted of them. Therefore in haft he dipatched away a Messenger with Letters to his Son, commanding him by the authority of a father to meet him at a certain day appointed at the City of *Verona* in the dominion of the *Venetians*; at which Town he promised to stay for him, as he went toward *Germany* to the Emperor: and for his sons more security, he procured a safe conduct from the Duke and Seignory of *Venice*, that his son might go and come without danger of life, or liberty. *Galeacius* receiving the letters, and being resolved by his own conscience, and them to whom he imparted the matter, that he might not any way with good conscience disobey so reasonable a request and lawfull a commandment of his father, answered that he would go; although he feared that by his meeting, and talk of his father and him, his fathers mind would but be more vehemently exasperate against him: for he firmly resolved afore he went, that all the threatnings, entreaties, counsels, and temptations that his father could devise, should not stir him one inch from that course of Religion, whereby he had begun to serve the Lord. With this purpose he departed *Geneva*, *Aprilis* 19. 1553. furnished with heavenly fortitude, assisted with the prayers of the Church, and armed with constancy, and with the sword of Gods word; whereby he hoped to sustain and beat back all the darts of temptations, whereby he knew he should be assaulted. Coming to *Verona*, there he found the Marquess his father, who received and used him kindly, though he could not but manifest in his countenance the inward anger and grief of his heart. After a few salutations

tations, the father began with all his cunning to deal with him about his return home again, laying open to the full that perpetual infamy, which was sure to fall on his house and posterity, unless that *Galeacius* did prevent so great a mischief: which (saith he) thou easily mayest do, and of right thou oughtest to do, and I know thou wilt do, if there be in thee but one spark of natural affection to father, wife, or children. *Galeacius* the son with such reverence as was due to his father, answered with all submission, that his body and estate is his fathers, but his conscience is the Lords: and tells him he can by no means return home, but he should make shipwrack of a good conscience: he proves it to him by good reasons, and such as his father could not resist,, and therefore humbly intreats his father, that seeing his desire is only to obey the Lord, and save his soul: that therefore he would not urge him to respect more the good estate of his children, than the glory of God, and his own souls health. The Marquess perceived he laboured in vain to remove his son from his resolution, which he judged to be nothing but a perverse stubbornness against the Catholick Religion, as he thought: and there-

therefore with grief of mind ceased that suit, and imparted to him the cause of his journey to the Emperor; strictly enjoyning him that he should not return to *Geneva,* but abide in *Italy* till he had obtain'd his suit at the Emperors hand, and was returned out of *Germany*; which thing *Galeacius* promised and performed; for he abode in *Italy* untill *August*: at which time he had notice that his father had prevailed in his suit before the Emperor. During which time, one *Hieronimus Fracastorius,* a notable Philosopher, Physician, and Poet, (being procured and set on by the Marquess) dealt with *Galeacius* with all his might and eloquence, to perswade him to yield to his father; adding withall, that that new Sect (as he term'd it) was false and deceitfull, and not worthy to be believed. *Galeacius* heard all he could say, and answered him point by point: and finally, by the pure simplicity of the word of God, he satisfied him (though he was both wise and learned) that he willingly held his tongue; and at last friendly intreated him, that he would not be angry for that his importunity and boldness with him.

CHAP.

CAAP. XVII.

Of his return to Geneva : *where he founded and setled a form of discipline in the* Italian *Church.*

THus *Galeacius* hearing of his fathers succefs, returned with a joyful heart toward *Geneva*; for that he saw his father delivered from the fear of that infamy, which the confifcation of his goods, and forfeiture of his lands, might have brought upon his family: and therefore he hoped he would be the lefs moved againft him. Whereupon fetling himfelf down again at *Geneva*, and devifing how to fpend his time in doing good, he began to confider ferioufly of fetling the difcipline in the Church of the *Italians* which was then at *Geneva*, (for thither had a great number of *Italians* tranfported themfelves and their families for Religions fake, flying the tyranny of the unholy Inquifition) and about that time it fell out fitly, that *Calvine* going Ambaffador from *Geneva* to *Bafil* in cafes

of Religion and other matters; entreated *Galeacius* to bear him company: whereunto he willingly condescended. At *Basil* he found an *Italian* called *Celsas*, whose right name was *Maximilian*, and was defended of the noble house of the Earls of *Mortinengo* in *Italy*: this man had got a great name in *Italy* among the Papists for his eloqvence and speech, and lately by the mercy of God was escaped out of the mire of Popish superstitions. *Galeacius* right glad of him, perswaded him to break off the purpose that he had for *England*, and go to *Geneva* with him, where he might live in the fellowship of a great number of his Countreymen, *Italians*, and enjoy the benefit of the company, conference and familiarity of many worthy men, but especially the most sweet acquaintance of that great *Calvine*: and all those with the liberty of a good conscience. The good Gentleman yeilded, and so they coming to *Geneva* by their industry with good means (together with the help and direction of *Calvine* in all things) that form of discipline was established in the *Italian* Church, which at this day standeth and flourisheth in the same Church, and remaineth recorded in a book for that purpose: and *Maximilian* the Earl, of whom we spake afore, was the first Pastor elect of
that

that Church, and undertook the charge, purely to expound the word of God, and to administer the Sacraments that Christ left behind him, and to watch over that flock and people: certain Elders were joyned as assistant to him, to whom was committed the care of the Church, to look to the purity of Doctrine and life in all estates; the principal of the Elders was *Galeacius* himself, unto whom the honour is due of bringing to pass so worthy an enterprise, and the rather for that by his authority, diligence, and watchfull care, he preserved the same in good and sure estate all his life-time; and after him it hath continued, being derived to others, to the great good and profit of many souls. And thus he passed this year 1554. with joy and comfort.

CHAP. XVIII.

The third contemplation to draw him away: liberty of conscience offered him by his Uncle Pope Paul the fourth: which after many temptations of flesh and blood to the contrary, at the last by the assistance of Gods grace he refused.

NExt succeeded in order the year 1555. wherein Satan assaulted him with new stratagems and devices: for that year his Uncle, which was *Paulus Quartus*, his mothers brother, attained the seat of the Papacy at *Rome*, whereby the Marquess his father conceived good hope by this means, either to draw his son home again, or at least to procure him liberty of conscience, and leave to live in some City of *Italy*, where he might enjoy the society of his wife and children, and they of him: Whereupon having occasion of business to travel that way, he sent letters to his son to *Geneva*, commanding him to meet him at *Mantua*

tua in *Italy*; and for his easier dispatch he sent him provision of money for the journey, *Galeacius* obeying again his fathers will, took his journey from *Geneva*, and came to *Mantua* the fifteenth of *June*, where he was entertained by his father with more then ordinary kindness, and in more loving manner then heretofore was accustomed. And at last he opened his mind unto him, the substance and effect whereof was, that he had obtained of his Uncle, who now was Pope, a dispensation for him; whereby liberty was granted him, to live in any City within the Jurisdiction of the *Venetians*, wheresoever he would, without any molestation to be offered him about his Religion or Conscience. His father tells him that if he do this, this will be a greater solace to his old age, than his departure and absense hath been grief unto him: besides all this, the good old man most earnestly intreated him (though he was the father, and spake to the son) that he would gratify him in this his request: and added many beseechings, who in any lawfull thing might by his authority have commanded him: and every word that he spake was so seasoned, as coming from the affection of a father; and at last with many strong reasons

sons persswaded him not to reject this so extraordinary a favour offered him by the Pope in so special and rare clemency, whereby he might without hurt of his conscience, live more commodiously than ever afore, and be restored to his former honour, and place, and estate; and recover the former love and estimation of all his friends, yea and of many strangers, who hearing of this his obedience to his father, would love him for it; unto which obedience to me (saith the father to his son) thou art bound both by the bond of nature, and by the law and word of God, which thou so much talkest of and urgest to me: therefore, saith he, if there be in thee either spark of natural affection, or any Religion and conscience of thy duty, thou wilt yeild unto me in this, especially seeing thou mayest do it without hurt or endangering of thy Conscience and Religion. This talk and request of the Marquess diversly affected *Galeacius*: for the thing he requested and the reasons he urged seemeed to be such as he could with no good reason contradict them; and yet he durst not presently entertain the motion; besides that the presence, authority, and reverend regard of his father, the vehemency and affection of his mind, and especially

cially the natural bond and obligation, wherein the son stands tied to the father in things lawfull and indifferent (especially when by that obedience no violence is offered to a good conscience) all these did greatly move him. Also natural and carnal reason for their parts assault him no less violently with such kind of arguments, as for the most part prevail with all men. For his father offered him yearly revenues, competent and fit for his estate, the solace of his children, and society of his wife: which two things he desired above all other things in the world, So that to this motion and request of his father the Marquess, *Galeacius* knew not well what to answer on a sudden; but stood for a time musing and doubting what to say; and the rather, for that he then wanted his special friend, faithfull *Calvine*, with whom he might consult in so weighty a cause: It seemed to him impious and ungodly, not to yeild to his father in so lawfull and reasonable a request, and he saw no way how he might deny it, but must needs incurr and undergo his fathers extream displeasure: and yet how he might yeild to it with safety of conscience he much doubted; for he feared that more danger to his profession and

and Religion, and consequently more hur[t]
to his soul might hereupon ensue then h[e]
could perceive: so that he stood altogethe[r]
unresolved in his own reason what to do
therefore in this extremity he denied him
self, and renounced his own wit, and i[n]
humble and fervent prayer betook himsel[f]
in this difficulty to the blessing and direction of his God and Saviour, the author an[d]
true fountain of Wisdom and constancy
humbly craving of the Lord to assist hi[m]
with his holy Spirit, that in this extremit[y]
he might advice and resolve of the best an[d]
safest course, for Gods glory and his ow[n]
found comfort. (O how truly sung that
sweet singer of *Israel* King *David*, when he
said, *How happy and blessed are they that fear God, for God will teach them the way they should walk!*) *Galeacius* found it most true
in his own experience; for upon this his
submission and prayer, the Lord from heaven resolved him in this sort, That seeing
the Pope did (Antichrist-like) directly op-
pose himself to Christ, and his Religion
and Church; that therefore he might by
no means sue for, or accept any favour at
his hand, not be by any means beholding
to him at all. Because what shew of service
soever was done to him by the enemy of
Christ,

Chrift, feemed to be taken from Chrift himfelf. Further, Gods fpirit perfwaded him it carried too great a fhew of Apoftacy, of backfliding, to forfake the company of godly profeffors, and the fellowfhip of Chrifts Church ; and to live amongft Idolaters in the middeft of all abominations. The fame fpirit of God fet before his eyes that fcandal and offence which this fact of his would breed in the minds of the faithfull, which would think that he had taken his farewell of Religion, and would now fhake hands, and renew his acquaintance with his old friend the world : that he had lightly efteemed the fpiritual bleffings and heavenly jewels of graces, which God diftributed daily in his Church ; and would now betake himfelf again to the old affections of his flefh. The fame fpirit refolved him, that thus to forfake the ordinary means, and deprive himfelf of the true ufe of the Word and Sacraments, and to live in a place where was nothing but Idolatry, was to tempt God in the higheft degree. God likewife opened his eyes, that he perceived the fleights of Satan by this his fathers drift : namely, to entangle him again in the net of worldly cares, to wrap his mind in the fnares of *Italian* pleafures ; and

and so dazle his eyes with the honours, and pleasures, and sensual delights, which once he had been brought up in, that his Religion might decay by little and little; and that all godliness might by the heat of these new pleasures, fall and melt away, like as wax before the fire: and lastly, the Lord upon his prayer granted him the wisdom of his holy spirit, to answer all his fathers objections, and confute all his arguments. And amongst many other, he earnestly entreated his father, that he would not do that unto him, which afterward he would repent that ever he had done: namely, that he would not be a means to make him a prey to the Papists; which had confirmed for a Law, and ratified it by many examples, that promise, faith, nor oath, is to be kept with any man whom they call Hereticks. Whereupon, said he, It is better for me, and more joy to you, to live as I do with the poor estate, then with hope of better to endanger my life, and so our whole posterity. By these, and such like perswasions it pleased God so to work upon the Marquess; that he was overcome in this suit, wherein he supposed to have prevailed; and therefore he yeilded against his will: and so with a sorrowfull heart he returned to *Na-ples*:

ples. And as he went, he certified the Pope of the obstinacy of his Son, and so the father and the uncle bewailed together their ill success.

CHAP. XIX.

Of his acquaintance with Franciscus Portus, *and the religious Dutchess of Ferrara, in his return home to* Geneva.

BUT in the mean time *Galeacius* after he had accompanied his father somewhat on the way, returned with a full glad heart, and came to the City of *Ferrara*: where he was joyfully received of *Franciscus Portus* a noble and renowned man for learning, and who afterwards taught publickly at *Geneva* many years, and read the Greek Lecture with great profit to the audience, and praise to himself. This *Portus* brought *Galeacius* into acquaintance with the noble Dutchess of *Ferrara*, who entertained him honourably, and after much conference had with him of the alteration of his Religion, of the success of his long voyages and tedious journeys, of the Church of *Geneva*, of

G   *Calvin,*

Calvin, and of many chief points of Christian Religion; she dismissed him, and left him to his journey; but not without all courtesies that she could afford him: and namely for one, to relieve the length and tediousness of the way, she lent him her own Chariot: and thus *Galeacius* was conveyed in the Chariot of so great a Princess as far as to the Town of *Francolium*: from whence having a pleasant Tide down to the River of *Po*, or *Padus*, he came by water into *Venice*: where taking ship and crossing the sea, he went thorow *Switzerland* to *Geneva*, and thither came the fourteenth of *October* in the same year; the whole congregation, and especially his chief friends, rejoycing with joy unspeakable for the safety of his return. And thus this cruel tempest being overblown, and now quieted, and Satan seeing he prevailed not by any of those forcible assaults, yet thought to try him with one more, and therefore came upon him afresh, like as a second fit of an Ague, stronger then the first: and by this Satan feared not but to give him the overthrow, and to bring him home again into *Italy*: and thus it was.

CHAP.

CHAP. XX.

The fourth assault, that Satan used to him back again, was by his wife, who by her letters won him to come and meet her in Italy, which he yeilded unto, and gave her a meeting.

His wife *Victoria* burned in long love and hearty affection toward her husband *Galeacius*, so that it cannot be uttered how vehemently she desired his company, whereupon she never ceased writing to him, and intreating him to return again to her and his children. But when she saw her womanly arguments and vain scribbling did no good, at last she in an earnest manner desired him to meet her in some City within the Territory of the *Venetians*, not far from the Kingdom of *Naples*. To this motion *Galeacius* yeilded: and thus the husband and wife promised to meet; but the ends that they aimed at were divers: she hoped by her flattery and fair speeches, her tears, and lamentations, to win her husband home

home again; on the other fide he was much more bufie in devifing how he might perfwade her to deliver her felf out of the filth of Popery, and come and dwell with him. With thefe refolutions they both going forward, fhe came to *Vico*, to her father in law the Marquefs; he came from *Geneva* to *Lafina*, a City in *Dalmathia*. This *Lafina* is diftant from *Vicum* an hundred *Italian* miles by water; and ftandeth juft over againft *Vicum*: and the fea called the *Venetian* Gulf lyeth betwixt them. *Galeacius* here abode, and exfpected his wife: but at that time fhe came not as fhe had promifed, and he expected. Yet he could never learn the caufe of her ftaying at that time, nor what it was that moved her fo to difappoint him; yet though fhe came not her felf, fhe fent two of her eldeft fons to their father; whofe fight was moft welcome, and their company moft comfortable to *Galeacius*: but on the other fide it grieved him the more; becaufe the fight and company of his wife was abfent, efpecially for whom he had taken fo long a journey: therefore fending them foon after home again, he went away forrowfull to *Geneva*. Where he had refted but a few days, but another packet of letters came pofting from his wife, befeeching beseeching him not to think much at her former negligence, and to vouchsafe once again to come to the same place: where, without fail, she would most gladly attend him, and solemnly vowed with large protestations she would not disappoint him. The request was very unreasonable, and it was a hard case for *Galeacius* thus to spend his time, and weary his mind and body in so long and dangerous journeys, and to so little purpose as hitherto he had. Notwithstanding, one thing moved him to yield even to this motion also; namely, a perswasion that he had, that when he first forsook his Country, he did not fully discharge his duty, in labouring to win his wife to have gon along with him; by explaining to her the chief heads of Christian doctrine, whereby she might possibly have received some taste, and so have taken some liking of true Religion; desiring therefore now, if it were possible to make amends for his former negligence, he yielded to go. And so obtained for his better security in going and returning a pasport or safe conduct from the high Court of *Rhætia*; he departed from *Geneva* the seventh of *March*, in the year 1558. and came to *Lesina* in *Dalmathia*, over against *Vicum*: where he had intelligence that the Marquess

quess his father, his wife his children, and his uncles son (he of whom we heard before) were already come to *Vicum*, with purpose to have been by that time at *Lasina* with *Galeacius*; but they could not, by reason that a Mariner of *Venice* had broken promise with them, and disappointed them: by reason whereof, and of other dangers of the sea, they could not as yet take shipping, nor durst venture over the Water. Whereupon *Galeacius* not induring patiently so long delays, resolved to go himself over to *Vicum*. Such was his faith in thee Lord, and his love to his friends, that he respected not the imminent danger, but constantly relied on the Lords protection; knowing that no fleshly affections drove him to this journey, but a sincere zeal to Gods honour, and the souls health of his kindred, and the discharging of his own duty unto them; whereunto he was perswaded that he had special calling.

CHAP.

CHAP. XXI.

Of his arival at Vico, *his fathers chief house, and his entertanment there: and what means were used to seduce him: and how his wife refused not only to go with him, but even to lie with him, because he was an Heretick: being thereto, as she said commanded by her Confessor.*

AND so arriving by Gods mercy on the coast of *Italy*, not far from *Vicum*, he gave intelligence of his approach to his father the Marquess; who presently sent his children to meet their father: and all his retinue to attend him into the Castle; at whose entrance it cannot be expressed how great joy was in all that house and noble family: and how all the Nobles and Gentlemen of his kindred and acquaintance rejoyced at his return; and began to cheer up their hearts with a new hope, which hitherto had been cast down and oppressed

with grief and despair. But above all other his wife (Madam *Victoria*) surpassed in joy and new conceived delight; hoping she had now recovered her most dear Lord and beloved husband, the only comfort and the sweet solace of her life. All (but *Galeacius*) exceedingly rejoyced at this meeting here; though indeed it greatly joyed his natural affection, to enjoy the company of his friends, so many, so near, and so dear unto him: yet his joy was tempered and allayed with a certain doubting fear which ran in his mind night and day. For the wise Gentleman well foresaw, that the fruition of that pleasure was but to last a while, and soon would have an end; for the end of his coming was not that which they imagined: and every day new matters ran in his head, the consideration whereof did not a little trouble him. He hath often since discoursed unto his friends, that all those days he lived in continual fear, to be suddenly apprehended, and cast into some filthy prison, where he should spend his days in languishing and lamentations, without any solace of his friends: yea and be utterly debarred of the comfortable reading of Gods holy word: but to return to the matter. At his first arrival he was entertained with
much

much joy on all sides, and many cheerful countenances and kind welcomes. But alas! within a few days all his mirth and joy was turned into tears and lamentation, and unmeasurable grief: for when once he had opened to his father the Marquess his constant purpose to persevere in the truth of that Religion he had begun to profess; and that he would rather dye in the defence of it, than to be drawn from it; then alas, what sighing, what crying, yea what dolefull lamentation did it move in them all! But then let the Christian Reader judg what a troubled spirit and wofull heart that good man had in this so fearfull a combate betwixt the grace of God and his natural affections; and what a torment it was unto him, to see them all so near and dear unto him, labour to withdraw him from God; and to see his constancy in Religion so to grieve them, which was the joy of his own heart. Yet taking up with himself as well as nature could, and comforting himself in his God, he afterwards dealt with his wife in all loving and yet earnest manner that she would follow him her husband, and delay no longer time; but come and live with him according as the Law of God and nature required: which if she
would

would do, he promised her liberty of her Conscience and Religion, to live as she would. But for his own part, he told her aforehand, as she should after find; namely, that he was firmly resolved to live and dye in that Religion, which (by the hand of God leading him) he had undertaken; and for the which he had forsaken Country, kindred, and all those excellent and comfortable blessings of this life, which God had given him. Here I leave it to the Reader but especially to the hearts of such women, as being wives, do truly love their husbands, to judg with what sobs and heart-breakings the silly Gentlewoman heard these words of her husband, whom she now saw past all hope to be perswaded to stay with her; which she desired above all worldly things. Yet it appeares it was but in meer carnal and worldly respects, as the consequent shewed: for though she loved him and desired his company never so much; yet being a wife, worldly, wilfull, and indeed a right Papist, she answered him plainly (though with many tears) that she would never go with him to *Geneva*, nor to any other place, where was any other Religion but that of *Rome*; and that she would not live with him as long as he was

was intangled with those heresies (as she called them) whereby it appears that she was a carnal politick Papist. She loved him, but where? in *Italy*; and there would live with him, but not at *Geneva*: and why? for in *Italy* he might advance her to the state of a Marchioness, in *Geneva* he could not: there she might live with him a life full of all delights; but in *Geneva* a hard, base, and obscure life, and subject to many outward dangers and miseries; In which respects it was that she was so instant upon him to stay with her. But the conclusion was, her desire was to enjoy him and *Italy* both; but rather then she would leave *Italy* and the delicacies thereof, she chose plainly to forsake him, and to withdraw the duty of a wife from him. For it may in no case be omitted (which afterward he imparted to some, his interest and most inward friends) that she even then and there denyed him that duty which a wife is bound to yield to her husband by the Law of God and nature: that is, she would by no means give him due benevolence, nor consent to lye with him as man and wife: and gave this reason, that she was expresly forbidden of her Confessor, under pain of excommunication, because he was an Heretick.

tick. Where behold Popish Religion what it is that can separate man and wife for disparity in Religion; and can discharge men and women from those duties of marriage with which God hath charged them. How this monstrous unkindness and unwomanly answer pierced his heart, let any Christian man judg, whom God hath honoured to be an husband. Yet he overcame and even devoured all these tormenting griefs, and bare them with an invincible constancy and quietness of mind. Yet he purposed not to bear so great an injury for ever; but to redress and help it if it were possible: and therefore he further proceeded with her, and openly and plainly denounced to her, that unless she would yield him that matrimonial duty, which by Gods law she ought, namely to eat, & lie, and live with him: it would be a cause to make him sue out a divorse against her, and so procure a final separation; which if she were the cause of, she might thank or rather blame her self, who withdrew her neck from the yoke of duty towards him which marriage required, and which he for his part said he would never have done to her, though her Religion was so far differing from his. Yet notwithstanding he said, that she first refusing him, he had then just cause to refuse her, who
had

had first by refusal of that duty refused her self as it were, and denied her self to be his wife. And so he concluded with her, that unless she would be his wife, he would no longer be her husband. This protestation no doubt amazed and troubled her not a little, and vexed the womans mind; especially for that he was and had always been such a husband to her, so good and kind, and every way so well deserving, that she loved him as her own eyes, (therfore more was she to blame that she esteemed him not as the light of her eyes:) but though this troubled her sore, yet it moved her not to her her duty; so good a scholar was she in this Popish learning, that she would rather incur her husbands, yea Gods displeasure than her Confessors; and rather break their commandment so holy and just, than his, which was so ungodly, and so unreasonable: and it also less prevailed with her because she imagin'd he would not so do (though he spake so) but only did it to fear her, and so in fear hereof to make her yield unto him.

CHAP.

CHAP. XXII.

Seeing he could not reclaim his Lady, he resolved to return to Geneva: *and of the grievous temptations he indured: where he took his last farewell of his father, wife, children, and friends: and of his heavenly courage, in bearing and passing through them all.*

When therefore the good Gentleman saw all things so far amiss, that even his wife was against him of all other, and gave him a deeper wound than all other his friends; denying him that society and fellowship which the bond of marriage yieldeth, and seeing that the time passed without any good doing, but rather to the increasing of his grief on all sides; he therefore resolved to depart, and so calling his wife *Victoria* again, he iterated unto her his former protestation; and so bad her take it at his last warning. The dolefull day of his departing being come, he held on

Galeacius takes his last farewell
his father, wife, children, and friends.

p. 94

on his purpose, and so entered into the Chamber of his father the Marquess to do his duty unto him, and to take his leave: who seeing his son thus past all hope of recovery, quenching his fatherly affection in fury and raging madness, like a frantick or desperate man, reviled him in most despightfull terms: and at last gives him his farewell with many a heavy and bitter curse. This so strange and extraordinary persecution did this good Gentleman suffer for Chrifts sake; and it is marvail that it did not cause him to look back again, and turn his course. But it was Gods doings that his father should use these extream and violent curses, rather then to go about to win him by allurements and gentle perswasions, for he hath often used to tell his friends, that this monstrous inhumanity and unnaturalness of his father did rather confirm and settle his mind; his nature being rather to be led than drawn, and rather to be won by friendliness and fair means, than to be urged by extremities. But God would have his servant to be tried by both means: namely, the allurements of his wife, and the menacings of his father. Thus God would purge him in the fire of all kind of temptations. And thus by the power of Gods grace

grace having passed thorough
hold hotter is to be ventured
ing his fathers Chamber, with
of curses (which the Lord turn
sings) he came into the great C
so into the Hall; where he fou
his children, his Uncles son (
of) divers noble Gentlemen h
and some of his ancient famil
mestick friends: all fraught
and making heavy chear;
heard but sighs, and sobbs, an
thing was seen but tears and
hands: his wife embracing him
him about the neck, beseeched
loving and most pittifull mann
would have care of himself, of
all his children, and whole hou
so willingly to cast them all
young children all upon their
armes streatched out, and hand
and faces swoln with tears,
him to have pity on them his o
and not to make them fatherless
time. His cosen and other ki
heavy countenance and watry
rufully on him; and though for
were not able to speak one wo
yet every look, and every coun

every gesture was a loud cry, and a strong intreaty that he would stay, and not leave so antient and noble a house in such wofull and desolate case. No words can suffice to express the grief of that dolefull company, nor that lamentable departure that there was to be seen. Unutterable was the grief on their side, and unspeakable was the torment and temptation which the noble Gentleman felt in this agony, when he must either leave Christ Jesus, or leave all these for him; but amongst and above all, there was one most lamentable sight, which would even have wrung tears from a heart of flint. Amongst all his children he had one daughter, a towardly and goodly young Gentlewoman of twelve years old, who crying out amain, and wallowing in tears, fell down, and catching fast hold about his thighs and knees, held him so hard as he could by no means shake her off; and the affection of a Father wrought so with him, as he could not offer with violence to hurt her; he laboured to be loose, but she held faster; he went away, but she trailed after, crying to him not to be so cruel to her his child, who came into the world by him. This so wonderfully wrought with his nature, he being a man of a most loving and kind affection, that he hath often reported he thought that his bowels rolled about within him, and that his heart would have burst presently, and there instantly have died, his child so having him fast about the legs. But notwithstanding all this, he being armed with a supernatural and heavenly fortitude, he brake thorow all these temptations, and treading under foot whatsoever might hinder him from Christ, he escaped out of this perilous battel a glorious conquerour; and so leaving that sorrowful house and dolorous company, he came with speed to the shore, where presently taking shipping, he caused them to hoist up sails towards *Lafina*, with a turmoiled and distressed mind, one way surcharged with sorrow to remember the manner of his departure, another way surprized with joy to remember that he had escaped. And even as a ship in a tempestuous Sea, the boisterous waves tossing it up and down, is thrown about, sometime touching the clouds, sometime plunged into the deep: So no doubt the noble mind of this young Marquess was no less distracted with contrary cogitations, being as it were in a labyrinth of distempered affections: sometimes he could

not

not but remember that lamentable estate wherein he left his Father, Wife and Children; he often imagined he was still amongst them; he thought he heard them cry and call upon him, he thought he still felt his dear daughter clasping him about the legs, and trailing after him; neither could he contain but break out into tears, neither could he for his life but often look back at that Princely house, with all those goodly Orchards, Gardens, Granges, Fields, and Territories, to all which he was heir apparent; yet all which he saw he must leave for Christ's sake. But one thing pierced his heart, to see his Wife and Children, and other his alliance standing on the shore, who when they could not speak to him, looked at him; and when they could not see him, ceased not to look after the ship as long as it was in sight; neither could he refrain but with a woful countenance look at them again as long as he could discern them; and withall he called to mind the bitter words and heavy farewell which the Marquess his Father gave him at his departure; all which cogitations running in his head, did doubtless wring from his sorrowfull heart many a deep sigh and heavy groan, and many a bitter

ter tears from his watery eyes; and yet notwithstanding all these, the spiritual strength and courage of his mind was constant and invincible. And even as a good Pilot in a raging Sea, when clouds and darkness, thunder and lightnings, storm and tempest run together, and toss the ship from wave to wave, as lightly as a ball from hand to hand; yet for all that he sits still at the helm, with undaunted courage, and marks his Compass; and by his courage and skill together, keeps on his right and stedfast course thorow all the rage of sea and weather; even so this our thrice noble *Galeacius*, taking hold of the holy and heavenly anchor, namely, a lively faith in Christ, and stedfast hope in God, he surmounts the clouds, and fixeth those anchor-holds in Heaven, and looking stedfastly with a spiritual eye at the true load-star, namely, Christ Jesus, and the hope of eternal happiness, he directs his course towards the same with an heroical spirit, and heavenly resolution, thorow the tempestuous waves of those fearfull temptations; and the ship that carried his body, did not so fast transport him from delicate *Italy* towards *Dalmatia*, as the ship of heavenly constancy and love of God withdrew his mind, and medi-

meditation from all natural respects and worldly delights, and made it mount aloft in holy contemplation. And thus the presence and grace of God's spirit having overcome the power of natural affections, he began to chear up himself after this tempest; and first of all, bending the knees of his heart to the eternal Father in Heaven, he yielded his Majesty most hearty thanks, for that he had furnished his soul with such a portion of his grace, as to withstand and conquer Satan in such a perilous battel; and for that he had delivered him from the danger of Popish thraldome, from the Inquisition, and from that perpetual imprisonment both of conscience and body which the Popish Church would have brought him unto, had he not thus escaped their hands. He likewise praised God unfainedly, that he vouchsafed to give him time, opportunity and grace to discharge that duty to his Wife the young Marchioness, which at his first departure he had omitted, and which oftentimes he had with great grief bewailed; and that he had enabled him to omit nothing which might have perswaded her to have left *Sodom*, and to have undertaken with him this blessed Pilgrimage towards the heavenly *Jerusalem*,

lem. The remembrance of thefe things much refrefhed his troubled mind. It alfo much contented and fatisfied his confcience, that upon that monftrous and undutifull behaviour of his Wife towards him (fpoken of before) he had made that proteftation which he did; namely, that he would ufe the lawful means to be divorced from her, who had firft of all divorced and cut off her felf from him, by denying that duty of love which the Wife may not deny to the Husband, nor the Husband to the Wife; he perfwaded himfelf that this proteftation would work well with her, and make her more conformable to her duty, when fhe had advifedly thought of it.

CHAP.

CHAP. XXIII.

Of his Journey home again by Venice, *and thorow* Rœtia *and* Switzerland; *and his safe arrival at* Geneva; *and of the great joy he brought to the Church by his safe return.*

REviving his troubled spirits with these cogitations, he arrived at *Lesina* in *Dalmatia*, which is the Countrey over against *Italy*, from whence he passed in a very quiet passage and calm Sea to *Venice*, where he found many faithful servants of God, and good Christians; who having heard afore that he was gone to *Vicum*, were exceedingly afraid for that imminent and inevitable danger they saw he was in, either to have his conscience a slave to Popish vanity, or his person a Prisoner to Popish cruelty; therefore they ceased not to pray for him night and day; and yet for all that they feared greatly what would become of him. But when now at last they saw him return both found in conscience,

and

and safe in person, and such a glorious conquerour over Satan, and over so many strong temptations with which the world and natural affections had assailed him: their fear was turned into comfort their sorrow into joy, and they all glorified the Lord for him. And so after mutual comfort given and received, he departed from *Venice*, and travelled thorow *Rhætia* and *Switzerland*, where he visited the Churches of the Protestants, and comforted them greatly with his presence, and by telling them what great things the Lord had done for him; and so by the good hand of his God upon him, he came in safety to *Geneva* the fourth of *October* in the year 1558. His safe arrival brought exceeding joy to the whole Church there, but especially to the *Italian* Congregation; for his long absence had brought them unto some suspence and doubt, not of any alteration of his Religion, but of some cruel and false measures to have been offered him by the deceitfull Papists. But when they saw him so safely returned untoucht in conscience, and unhurt in his person, and that he had passed so many pikes of temptations which they knew had been pitched against him, they gave great thanks to the Lord for him. But when

when he had discoursed unto them particularly the whole course of the proceedings: first, what a strong battery of temptations and assaults the Devil and the World had planted against him, then how manfully he fought and withstood, and at last overcame them all; they fell into admiration of so rare constancy; and thought him worthy of all honour, to whom it is given (as the Apostle saith) to suffer so much for Christ and for Religions sake; and in all earnest manner they magnified the singular grace and mercy of God towards the whole Church in him, which had not suffered his servant (this noble *Galeacius*) to be seduced out of the way of that holy calling whereto the Lord had called him; and who had delivered him from so subtile a train, laid by the policy of the enemy Satan, to have intrapt his soul and conscience, by overturning him in the race of his Religion: and they all acknowledged that this noble and godly Gentleman found it verified in himself, which the Kingly Prophet saith in the Psalm: *Because he hath trusted in me, therefore I will set him free: I will be with him in his troubles, I will deliver him and crown him with honour:* and in another place, *He that trusteth in the Lord shall never be confounded.*

founded. And thus the Church received a double benefit by him; for first his practice was an example unto them all of a most extraordinary and heavenly constancy in the love and profession of true Religion; secondly, the mercifull dealing of the Lord with him, was a notable confirmation of their faith, and an encouragement to them to persevere and stand to the truth, with assurance that the Lord himself would stand by them.

CHAP. XXIV.

Certain years after his return to Geneva, he begins to feel in himself a necessity of marriage; he delivers his case to Calvin, *who refused to consent; the matter is referred to the Churches of* Switzerland, *and by them he is resolved that he is free from his first Wife, and may marry again.*

AND with an unspeakable contentment in his own conscience, and with publick joy and thanksgiving of the whole Church

Church, he settled himself at *Geneva* in his former private and quiet life. Where after a few years he began to finde in himself some reasons which perswaded him to think it needfull for him to live in the state of marriage; and therefore having thus long waited and expected a more wise and dutifull answer from his Wife, and perceiving by her not answering that she still persisted in that monstrous and annatural wilfulness, which her blinded Popish mind had formerly undertaken, by the perswasion of her blinded Popish guides; he therefore purposed to take such course for his remedy, as by the Law of God and his Church should in that case seem allowable; namely, to be divorced from her, who for her part had broken the bond, and untied the knot of matrimony. And first of all he imparted his mind and purpose to Mr. *Calvin*, and craved his godly and wholesome counsel in a case of so great importance. His counsel was first of all, that it was more convenient, and less scandalous to the enemies of Religion if he could abstain. But the Gentleman replied, that the case was so with him as he could not abstain, and gave him many weighty reasons which drew him to marriage; and withall participated unto him

him some secret reasons for the which he affirmed it was altogether necessary for him to marry. Holy *Calvin*, as he was a man endued from God with sharpness of judgement, and a wise and a discerning spirit; so he foresaw plainly that many would speak evil of the fact, others would take offence at it, some would plainly condemn it, and speak evil of Religion for it; and the rather, because (as he truly said) very few did rightly conceive the full truth in the doctrine of divorcement; but fewest of all would or could know the whole circumstance of this particular fact. He likewise wisely considered, that the like president was seldome seen, especially in the *Italian* Church, whereof this Gentleman was a principal member, and of special account both for his nobility, birth and descent, and for his zealous love to Religion. All which considerations, with divers other, made Reverend *Calvin* not too easily to subscribe to this purpose and motion of *Galeacius*. Notwithstanding, when the Gentleman urged him out of the word of God and good conscience, with arguments which he saw and confessed, he could not sufficiently answer; therefore lest he should burden and trouble the conscience of so

good

good a man, which alledged for himself, that he was driven by necessity to that course, he yielded thus far to him; that if he would repair unto the Learned and Reverend Divine *Peter Martyr*, and ask his opinion and the opinions of all the learned and chief Divines of *Rœtia* and *Switzerland*, and desire them seriously to consider of it, (as in a matter of such moment, and of so great consequence, it was requisite) and then set down their judgements in the matter, and the reasons moving them thereunto he promised that he would also subscribe unto them, and most willingly yield unto him what liberty soever they did allow him; alwaies provided that he also should submit himself unto their censure, and stand to the trial of their judgements in this case. *Galeacius* most willingly yielded hereunto, as one who desired nothing but that which the Lord by his Word, and by the voice of his Church should allow him; and so taking the course that *Calvin* had advised him, he caused Letters to be drawn and sent to *Zurich*, *Berne*, and other the Churches of *Switzerland*, opening the whole circumstance of the matter, and expounding the case truly and fully; and humbly craved the judgements of the Church

Church in a case of conscience so great and doubtful. The chief Preachers and most learned Divines yielded to his honest and godly request, and assembled about it; the matter was much and long debated, and argued at large on both sides; and after mature deliberation, and sufficient consultation had, it was concluded and agreed on by them all with one consent, that he might with safe conscience depart from that Wife, which had first of all on her own part broken the bond, and dissolved the marriage-knot; and for the proof of this their opinion, many causes and reasons were alledged and laid down out of the Scriptures, Fathers, Councils, and out of the Civil Law, which is the Law almost of all Countries in Christendom. All which (both of their conclusions and their reasons) were put in writing, and are registred and safely recorded, and are kept to this day ready to be shewed to whomsoever and whensoever need shall so require; for it was thought good by the Church so to do, both for that the case was extraordinary, and would be sinisterly spoken of and censured by many, who knew not sufficiently how it stood; and especially for the preventing of any slander or cavil which the enemies might object against our Religion.

CHAP.

CHAP. XXV.

By publick sentence of the Church, and judgement of the Law, he is divorced from his former Wife; and after a time he marrieth a French Gentle-woman, a widdow of about forty years of age, himself then being about three and forty.

Galeacius having thus laid his foundation, proceeded further, but still with the consent of the Church, and observing the due form of the Law, and the ordinary course of Justice in such cases, he craved publickly of the Magistrate that he might be divorced, that is, that he might be pronounced to be free, and discharged from that Wife, who had already cut off her self from him. The Magistrate considering the truth and circumstance of the case, together with the judgement of the Divines, where-unto also was agreeable the judgement of the Law, granted unto him as by his advo-
cates

cates it was required; and so in publick Court, and by sentence definite and irrevocable, he was divorced, and was pronounced to be free, and discharged of his former wife *Victoria*; and that it was lawfull for him, and in his choice, to live unmarried, or to marry as himself would. After which liberty obtained, he imparted the matter to his friends, and applied himself to think of another wife, he asked their advices in this point also. And herein he took that course which generally men in the world take not; for in his choice he respected not so much wealth, birth nor beauty, but only to find a fit companion of his life, and such a one, as with whom he might lead that which remained of his life in a comfortable contentment; in tranquillity of mind, and peace of conscience, that so he might the more chearfully serve the Lord, and wait for the coming of Jesus Christ. Which course of his is more to be noted, especially in so great a man, and so honourably discended; and the rather to cross and controll the carnal and worldly courses, which men for the most part, and women also, observe in their marriages; respecting those things first which should be last, and that last or not at all, which should be be first and above all. *Galeacius* continuing this his purpose, and looking about for his choice, the Providence of God (which doth never fail his Children, especially in so great matters) did offer unto him a fit oppertunity. For so it was, that at the same time, a certain Gentlewoman of *France*, a Widdow, came from *Roan* to *Geneva*, for true Religion sake, which she loved and professed, and for the love of it left her Country, and came thither for liberty of her conscience. She was a Matronly and grave Woman, and well reported of for her modesty, honesty, fear of God, and for manifold good qualities: Her name was *Anna Fremeria*, and was about forty years of age. All which circumstances *Galeacius* well observing, thought her a fit and convenient Wife for him: and so with the consent and liking of other his good friends, he took her to Wife, and married her the sixteenth day of *January* 1560. and in the three and fortieth year of his age; and they lived together many years after with much comfort one of another, and in an excellent agreement, being both of the same Religion, and of one mind; always drawing in one Yoke, and bearing one burthen, dividing it betwixt them;

whether

whether it was by joy or sorrow: so that the unquietness of life past, was now recompenced with a life full of all contentment; and so loving her, and being truly loved of her, they spent their days in all mutual comfort, solacing themselves in their quiet and private life, and joying in the mutual faithfulness and loyalty which one performed to another. Lo thus shall the man be blessed that feareth the Lord.

CHAP. XVI.

Of his course of life after his marriage; with his frugality.

NOW being married, he laboured to deliver and disburden himself of worldly cares; and therefore he prescribed to himself a sparing and frugal course of life; resolving to keep himself within the compass of his Revenue, which although it was as much again as it was afore, by his Wives Dowry, yet by many other hinderances was far less than heretofore it had been. And first for his Houshold, his care was to have
it

it as little as might be, and therefore for his service and attendance he only kept two maid-servants: and for himself he led his life in great sobriety, and in very mean estate, yet always free from sordid baseness, and always keeping a seemly decorum: never wanting any thing that was necessary, nor having much that was superfluous. His attire was plain and homely, but always comely, clean and handsome: and he that in his own Country might have been Lord of so many Tenants, and Commander of so many Servants, did now walk the streets of *Geneva* alone; often not having the attendance of one man: yea, he would not disdain to come himself into the market, nor think scorn to provide himself of necessaries; and sometime would buy and carry home fruits, herbs, roots, and such other things. And this course of Life, together with liberty of true Religion, he esteemed greater happiness than the Marquesdom of *Vicum*. And although by this course of Life he could scarce be discerned from an ordinary man, and from the common sort of people: notwithstanding in his countenance appeared that gravity, in his gestures, behaviours, and in his whole Body shone that comely Majesty, as any wife man to have seen him, and well considered him, would have presently judged that he came of a noble Race, and that he had been fit for the greatest employments of the world: which also was so much the greater, because that with his excellency of birth and person, and perfection of all Gentlemanly behaviours was joyned true godliness and the fear of God, which of it self is of such force; as it is able even to honour him, who wanted these worldly Ornaments and outward Perfections. How much therefore did it magnify him who had it in so great a measure, and accompanied with so many true Complements of Gentry and Honour? By all which it came to pass, that so many parts of the chiefest excellencies meeting in that one man, made him to shine above other the members of the Church, as the Moon among the Stars. So that the *Italian* Church, though but little of it self; yet by the vertues and worthiness of this one noble Gentleman, seemed to be compared with the whole Church of *Geneva*. And as he was an honour unto that Church, so was he again most honourably esteemed of that Church: yea, not only of that Church, but of the whole Church and State of *Geneva*: for not one Senator nor Magistrate

of

of the City, not one of the Preachers and Ministers of the Church was to be found, which had not always in their mouths the commendation of noble *Galeacius*: yea, he was honoured and highly esteemed of by them all, and it was hard to say, whether he was more loved or admired amongst them. In a word, he was loved of all men, looked at of all men, spoken of by all men, magnified and extolled, yea, wondred at of all men, and though he knew not many himself, yet all men laboured to know him. No publick meeting was appointed, no solemn Feast was made, whereto this our *Galeacius* was not solemnly called; yea, every man was desirous of him, and happy was he that might have his company: yea, they thought their meeting graced, and their houses honoured with his presence; and in all Assemblies the chiefest and highest Room was offered him, yea, was thrust upon him, though he nothing at all respected it. And although he refused the Name and Title of Marquess, because, he said, the Emperour had cut off his succession, and deprived him of that Honour, because of his Religion: notwithstanding, do what he could, he was called by no other means all his life long, and that not by some few, his friends and favourites,

but

but by all sorts of men, even strangers themselves, and such as were not of his Religion. For all men thinking that he had injury to be deprived of his lawfull succession; therefore though they could not give him the Living and Estate, yet they gave him all they could, that is, the Name and Title. Such were his Noble and Gentlemanly Qualities (besides his Christian Vertues) that they won the love and liking of all men; and caused them to honour him far above that he desired or cared for: yea, every one laboured to shew any service, or to perform any duty towards him: nay, strangers themselves were desirous to see him, and were drawn into admiration of him: insomuch, as whensoever any of the Nobility or Princes of Christendome, especially of *Italy*, did travel to see forreign Nations; and for the most part taking *Geneva* in their way (which place generally all Travellers have a great desire to see) they would by no means omit to see and visit *Galeacius*. Thus did *Francis* and *Alphonsus*, the young Dukes of *Ferrara*, *Octavius* the Prince of *Solerum*; and thus did *Fernesius* the Duke of *Parma*; and divers, who in their travel coming by *Geneva*, entertained him in all the Complements of Courtesie and of honour,

honour, no less than if he had been at *Naples* in his former glory: or if he had still been a Courtier in the Emperours Court, as heretofore he had been. In a word, no Noble Man, no Ambassadour, no great Scholar, no man of note of any forreign Nation came that way, but presently they used means to have a sight of this noble Marquess; and for the most part desired to have some company and conference with him: So that he was resorted unto continually by men of all sorts; as though he had not been a private man, keeping a mean estate and dwelling in a little house; but rather, as though he had been a Prince in the Court, or one near in place to the Emperour himself. But though all men desired his accquaintance and company, and he again was not curious in that point, but courteous to all as occasion was offered; yet for the most part, his most familiar conversation was with the men of his own Nation: namely, with his Country men the *Italians*, of whom there was a flourishing Church at *Geneva* at the same time; and which also flourished the better by his means, as heretofore hath been declared. Amongst whom though he behaved himself, it is doubtfull whether more civilly, or more humbly, yet for all that

that he was honoured of them all, and used more like a Lord than a private man: which although he in every respect deserved, yet by no means desired. And so besides all his worthy and excellent parts, his humble mind and friendly Conversation made him more honourable. And to speak but truth of him, out of all question he was not only a good Christian, but (which is not always seen) a perfect and an absolute man: yea, a man can hardly name any of these good parts, and amiable qualities, which for the most part do win a mans love in the world, which were not to be found in this noble Gentleman. For besides his Noble Birth and Princely Educations, his Religion and true fear of God, he was also humbly minded, affable, courteous, and friendly to all men: he was wise, discreet, of good conceit, and of an excellent speech and discourse. It would have delighted a man to have heard him speak; for as his Memory was exceeding good, so his natural Eloquence, his smooth stile, his easie, quiet, and seemly delivery, made his speech to be greatly commended of all that heard him. A man would have wondred to see how many even of the best sort, would have laboured to have been in his Company; and as

it

it were, hath catched up and eaten his words from his mouth: When it pleased him to discourse of some of those Exploits and Adventures, which had fallen within the compass of his own knowledg; as of the Emperor *Carles* the fifth his Voyage into *Provence*, and of his Wars which he waged in *Gelderland*, against the Duke of *Cleve*, and of many other great Affairs, and special Imployments. Neither was he only a fit Companion for Gentlemen and men of Estate, but such was the mildness of his nature and disposition, that he was also kind and courteous to men of lower place, and most of all to the poor; amongst whom, if they were godly and honest, he would converse as familiarly as with his Equals, or with men of greater place. He was also of a free and liberal heart; no poor or distressed man did ever require his assistance, or crave his help, but presently he would reach unto them by helping hand, and relieve them by all means he could; yea, the want of his former wealth, and loss of his Marquesdome did never grieve him, but when he had not wherewithall to exercise his Charity towards the poor souls of God: it was his joy and delight to be lending and giving to those that wanted, and in that respect only

he

he often wished himself as great a man in *Geneva*, as he was in *Italy*: but to his power and ability his good Works did far exceed the proud and Pharisaical Papists, who glory in their works, and will be saved by them. Prisoners and men in danger did often feel his bounty; he omitted not to visit his sick brethren, and that most diligently: such as were poor he relieved; yea, the richest and learnedst of all, did think themselves in their sicknesses happy to have him with them; his presence and company, but especially his talk and Christian exhortations were so comfortable unto them. His ordinary exercises were these: Every day he repaired to the Church, and heard divine Service, and missed not to be present at Prayers with the Congregation, especially he never omitted to hear the Sermons and the Word preached: which he did always with wonderfull Devotion and Reverence to the Word of God; for he judged and esteemed the true happiness of a man, and the only sweet and pleasant life consisted in living holily, in walking in God ways, in meeting with Satans temptations, in bridling the corruptions of his nature, and in serving God truly and sincerely without hypocrisie: unto all which

steps

steps of happiness he thought he could never attain, but by the preaching of the Word: whereupon he also adjoyned a daily course of reading the Scripture: thus labouring out of the Scriptures to lay the foundation of his own salvation, which he applyed to the profit and comfort, not of himself alone, but of many others with him.

Besides all this, for the love he bare unto the Church, and the desire he had to do all good he could; he took upon him the office of an Elder in the Church, the duty whereof he supplyed daily, carefully observing and inquiring into the manners and lives of Professors; allowing and encouraging the Good, and censuring the Offenders, which he did with great care and conscience, lest that scandals and offences might arise in the Church, whereby either the quiet and good estate of the Church at home might be disturbed, or the Enemy might have any occasion to slander the profession of Religion. Neither stayed he here, but beside this publick care and labour, he also was daily well occupied in more private matters: for whereever he saw, observed, or heard of any Dissentions, Suits in Law, or Controversies amongst Christian Neighbours,

bours, he was exceeding carefull to the end & compose them: and for that end, as he had a ripe wit, and a good conceit and deep insight, so he would employ them all to the finding out the truth and state of the cause: and having found it, he would use all his authority; yea, he would make himself beholding to men, on condition they would yield one to another, and live in peace. In a word, his whole course of life favoured of Grace, and did shew him to be a sanctified man; yet, doubtless, he thought himself born not for himself, but for God and for the Church: and he thought no time so well spent, nor any busines so well dispatched, as that wherein neither gain or pleasure to himself was thought or obtained, but only Gods glory advanced, his Church edified, Religion maintained, and the good work of Gods Grace confirmed in himself and others.

CHAP. XXVII.

Being aged, he falleth into a long and languishing sicknefs.

AND thus he lived at *Geneva* many years full of joy and quietnefs, comforts and contentment, far from all worldly ambition, and as it were forgetting what he was, and what he was born to in this World, only refpecting what he was to inherit in the world to come; and as he had begun, fo he continued in a loathing and deteftation of all Popifh fuperftition and impieties. But with this great quietnefs of mind and confcience, there wanted not fome outward and corporal vexatious: for after this long peace, new afflictions and ftorms came upon him, whereby the Almighty would the better try him, and make his faith, his hope, his patience and preferverance to fhine more glorioufly; that fo afterward he might receive a more excellent reward and a more glorious Crown.

For firft of all, he fell fick of a grievous doubtfull and dangerous Difeafe, which had

had bred upon him by abundance of rheume, whereby he became so short-winded that he could hardly draw his breath; by force of such weakness he was exceedingly tormented night and day: for the good Gentleman was constrained oftentimes to sit up whole nights together, and was fain to be removed from room to room, and from one place to another, to see if by any means he might take some sleep, which by the vehemency of this Disease was almost quite gone from him. This Disease had grown upon him by reason of his many, and long, and sore journeys, which he had taken by Sea and by Land for his conscience sake: and of the great Distempers and Alterations of the state of his Body, which for his Souls sake he had undergone.

CHAP.

A Jesuit is sent from his friends in Italy to reclaime him, by offering him great Summes of Money, etc: p.1.

CHAP. XXVIII.

A new temptation assaults him: a Jesuit is sent from his friends in Italy *to reclaim him by offering him great sums of money, and to make his younger son a Cardinal: but he valiantly scorneth it all, and sends him home back with shame.*

BUT this languishing sickness did not so much afflict his weak and aged body, as Satan laboured by another device, and a new temptation to trouble and vex his righteous soul. For it came to pass that about the same time when this disease had seized upon him, there came to *Geneva* out of *Italy* a Nephew of his, the natural son of his own sister, with letters to him from his former Wife *Victoria* the Marchioness, as also from his eldest Son the young Marquess: unto which letters this young Gentleman being a Scholar, added many words of his own to little purpose; labouring to perswade and allure him with
much

much and vain babling, that now at the last he would acknowledg. his errour, and return home again to his own Country, his former Religion, and his antient inheritance. The principal cause both of their writing, and his comming so far, was this; because, that if he would now at last return, hereby he might without doubt (as he said) advance his youngest son *Charles*, either to the Princely state of a Cardinal, or at least to be some great Bishop. For, saith he, whereas your Son is now admitted into Holy Orders, and is (for his great friends and alliance, and for his special towardliness) in possibility of so great preferment, your pertinacy and obstinate perversness in following and defending a new found and upstart Religion, and condemned (as he said) by all the great Estates of *Italy*, is the very hinderance of your Sons preferment. These kind of news, how highly they offended the holy and Christan soul of this thrice noble *Galeacius*, who from his heart abhorred, and in his soul detested those vain ungodly, and prophane Dignities in the Popish Church, I leave it to be judged by the Christian Reader; and therefore having with much grief of mind heard thus much of this unsavoury and unpleasant Message, and not able longer to forbear, he firſt of all took the Letters, and before his face that brought them; threw them into the fire; and then briefly, but gravely, wiſely, and zealouſly, he ſhaped him this anſwer by word of mouth, thinking ſo bad and baſe a meſſage unworthy the time and labour of writing. And firſt of all he told him, that there could not have come to him more heavy and unwelcome news of his Son than theſe; that he was ſo blind a Papiſt, that for the hope of this worldly advancement, he would venture the ruine and ſubverſion of his ſoul. And bad him tell his Son, that he would hinder him in that ungodly courſe by all means he could; and he ſaid, he knew not whether it more grieved him to ſee the vanity of his Sons proceeding, then it rejoyced him that it lay in his power any ways to hinder him in the ſame: Yea, ſaith he, know thou, and let that my ſeduced Son know, that you could have uſed ſcarce any argument unto me ſo forcible to make me perſiſt in my Religion, and to deteſt Popery, as this, that in ſo doing I may hinder my Son from the abominable dignities of the Popiſh Church; and therefore ſaith he, return my Son this anſwer, that inſtead of helping him to theſe preferments, I will pray for ever to the Lord for him, who is the Father

of his soul and mine, that he would open his eyes to see the truth, and that he may have grace after the example of me his Father, to see the horrible superstitious Idolatries and impieties of Popery, and seeing them to abhor and detest them, and renouncing the vanities of all worldly pomp and honour, to direct his footsteps to the Lord, and embrace his holy truth, and yield his soul and conscience obedient to the heavenly calling, and so become the servant and child of the most high God; whereby he may aspire and attain to the true and highest dignity, which is to enjoy the favour and comfortable presence of God, and his holy grace; to love God, and to be loved of him; and so at last to be advanced to that heavenly and eternal glory which is prepared for them, who in this world do forsake themselves and their own desires, that they may in true holiness serve the Lord. With these and such like holy speeches he answered the disholy and dishonest demand of this carnal Papist. But for all that, this importunate and unreasonable Jesuit (for he was of that Sect) ceased not to be troublesome to this Nobleman, still urging him with fond and frivolous reasons, and pressing him with ridiculous arguments; as this especially for one; he promised him a huge sum
of

of money if he would return home, which saith he lies ready at *Lions* for you, and the Brokers and Exchangers there are prepared to pay it. And he further assured him, that if he would come again into *Italy*, they had procured him liberty of his conscience and Religion at *Turing*; and there also (he said) he should find a great sum of money ready for him. But when this importunate fellow presumed to press the good conscience of this resolute Gentleman with such base arguments, and began to weigh Religion in a pair of gold weights, then the Noble heart of this holy Christian could not but shew it self moved, and therefore in a holy zeal and ardent love of his Saviour Christ Jesus, he cryed out, *Let their money perish with them, who esteem all the gold in the world worth one days society with Jesus Christ, and his holy Spirit:* and cursed, saith he, be that Religion for ever, which shall wed men to the world, and divorse them from God. Go home therefore, saith noble *Galeacius*, take away thy silver again, and make much of that dross of the earth, together with your dregs of Popery, lock them up together in the chest of your hearts. And as for me, know it, that my Lord and Saviour Christ hath made me enamoured of far more precious jewels, and durable riches;

riches; but the heavenly constancy of this holy man, drove this frantick Papist from his byass into an extream choller, for he according to the nature of his Popes holy Religion, thought that when all other arguments had failed, yet money would have won him, and therefore seeing him so highly to scorn, and so disdainfully to contemn the great offers, he thought it very strange; and therefore seeing all his labour lost, and his best hold prove so weak, he fell from money to meer madness; and forgetting himself and his duty, brake out into ill words, and reproachful terms: But when the Magistrates were informed of it, and saw that this arrogant Papist durst so far abuse the patience of so honourable a man, therefore by their authority they forbad him the City, (as the manner of the place is in such cases) and so this News-bringer had his Pass-port to be packing, and to go home and count his silver, and there to brag of his good success, for he now could say by good experience, that so much money as was enough to lead a hundred Popish Friers to and fro whether a man would, like Bears by the nose, could not touch the conscience of one Protestant, much less make him a Papist.

CHAP.

CHAP. XXVIII.

Being delivered from the importunity of the Jesuit; not long after came a Monk, nimble witted and learned, a kinsman of his own, who had a strong conceit he could have reclaimed him; but he came too late, the Marquess being dead before he came.

ANd thus it pleased God to deliver this sick Gentleman from this troublesome temper, and this Messenger of Satan which came to have buffeted him; but he buffeted him, yea and vanquished him, and Satan in him; that he might report at home, that he found the Marquess sick in body, but whole in mind, yea that he never saw in all his life so resolute a conscience, and so couragious a mind in so weak a body. And thus the Lord doubtless did in mercy to him, that being free from his disquiet companion, he might with more comfort and less grief bear the burden of his sickness, which now grew upon him more and more, and left him not till it made

him leave the world, and till it had translated him from this his pilgrimage to his eternal rest; and till it had made him of a poor Marquess upon earth, a glorious King in heaven. Whose death as it was wonderfully lamented of the Church for the unrecoverable loss they had of him, so it was a merciful blessing, and a welcome messenger of God to him: for it freed and delivered him from many storms of new temptaions which the Devil had raised against him; for within a short time after his death there came to *Geneva* a certain Monk, a good Schollar, a Gentleman by birth, and near akin to *Galeacius*, who being puft up with Monkish pride, and a conceit of his own ability for such an enterprize, thought so far to have prevailed with *Galeacius* by his nimble wit and eloquent tongue, as to have perswaded him now at the last either to have relinquished his Religion; or at least to have returned into *Italy*, (where his Uncle had been lately Pope) that so by his presence and countenance, and the help of his great friends, (which he had both in the Popes and Emperors Court) his children might be in more possibility of those high dignities and great places in the world, which they and their other friends aimed at; and for the attainment whereof nothing so much hindred
them

them as their Fathers Religion and course of life. But he returned home a proud Fool as he came, and ashamed of his proud and insolent spirit, which perswaded him by his vain babling he could have overcome him, whom he found when he came to *Geneva* to have overcome the world, and all spiritual enemies, and now to be triumphing in the glory of heaven. And so leaving him and all other his Popish and carnal kindred, gnashing their teeth for anger to see his admirable constancy; let us return again to our sick Gentleman, whose end now hasting on will also hasten an end to this strange story.

CAAP. XXX.

His long and languishing sickness grew and encreased upon him in such measure, as his pain was most grievous, but he bare it all with an heroical and heavenly courage; so that it might manifestly appear, that even the Lord from Heaven did lend him strength, and as the torments and pangs of the disease encreased, so his faith and patience, and all heavenly vertues shone in him more and more; so that it was most true of him

him which the Apostle saith, *as the outward man perisheth, so the inward man was renewed daily.* His body pined away, but his soul grew from strength to strength; and as a by-stander feels not the pains of him that is tormented or racked before his eyes; so his soul and mind stood as it were afar off, beholding the pains and vexations of the body, and being untoucht it self, did as it were laugh at Satan, sin, death, and damnation; who by all their joynt power could do no more, but only to vex and rack his poor carcass with bodily diseases, but were not able to touch the soul, to vex the mind, or wound the conscience. If any man ask the reason why his mind or conscience was so quiet in this so great torment of the body; the reason was, for that his mind was imployed in holy meditations, as of the singular love of God his Father unto him in Christ Jesus, whereby he assured himself undoubtedly of salvation, of the manifold holy graces wherewith God had adorned him; by the force whereof he said he had born off so many buffets of Satan, had passed so many pikes of troubles, and come away conqueror in so many fearful fights, as had opposed themselves against him in his conversion. These gifts and graces of God he weighed with the crosses of his sickness,

ness, and found them far heavier; and he compared these momentary and light afflictions, with that exceeding and eternal weight of glory which he said he knew was laid up for him in heaven. These and such like meditations cheared up his spirit more than the force of his sickness could appall him.

But above all things he felt unspeakable comfort and sweatness in his prayers to the Lord, which he poured out most fervently, and with a zealous and faithful heart; and would often say, that in the midst of his prayers his soul seemed to him to be even ravished out of himself, and to taste of the blessed joys of heaven. So that the saying of the blessed Apostle was verified in him: *As the sufferings of Christ abounded in us, so consolation by Christ abounded much more.* In his sickness he wanted no help of the Phisitians, for they came to him out of all parts of the City, and willingly did they all do their diligence about his body, whose soul they knew had Christ Jesus to be the Phisitian for it. His friends also continually visited him, who were of the chief men in the City; and they were all welcome to him, rich and poor: & it is hard to say whether he received more comfort by them, or they more spiritual edification by him; his speeches and behaviours were

were so full of patience, and so well seasoned with all grace. All his friends performed to him what duty soever was in their power, but especially his worthy Wife did then shew her self most loving and loyal, for she was never from about him, and saw that he wanted nothing which the world could yield for the recovery of his health. But all was in vain, for the time of his dissolution was at hand, and he had run the Royal Race of a most holy Christian life, and now nothing remaining but a blessed death. He might say as the Apostle did with much joy of heart, *I have run my race, I have finished my course, I have kept the faith; from henceforth is laid up for me a Crown of righteousness, which Christ the righteous Judg will give to me, and to all such as wait for his appearing.*

After few days the violence of his sickness was such, as it overcame all power of physick; so that it was manifest, that that blessed hour approached wherein the Lord had appointed to accomplish his own good work in him, therefore he sequestred himself from all care of his body, and from all worldly cogitations; he renounced the world, and all in it; he took his farewell of his Wife, and his Christian Friends, and said he should lead them the way to Heaven. He fixed all his thoughts

thoughts upon his soul, and soul and all on the Lord in heaven; and cryed to Christ Jesus, that as he had sought him all his life, so he would now receive him and acknowledg him for his own. And thus all his friends sat about him, and as the Preachers and Ministers were occupied in holy prayers, and reading of the holy Scriptures, and applying to him the heavenly consolations of Gods Word, in the performance of these exercises he ended his days, wherein he had taken delight all his life long; and as he rejoyced in them in his life, so it pleased the Lord that he should have them at his death. And so in the midst of all his Friends, in the presence of the Ministers, even in the sight of them all, he peaceably and quietly yielded up his spirit, and rendred his soul into the hands of the merciful God and faithfull Creator, of whom he had received it; who immediately by the Ministery of his holy Angels receiving it at his hands, washing it pure in the blood of Jesus Christ, crowned it with the crown of eternal and heavenly happiness. And thus this holy man was translated from a Nobleman of earth, to be a noble Saint in heaven; and of a Marquess on earth in bare name and title, he was advanced to be a glorious and triumphing King in heaven, where he now reigns in glory with that God whom he so faithfully served on earth. That God and merciful Father grant that all we that read this admirable story, may be allured to take upon us the same most holy profession that this thrice noble Marquess did; and may renounce and cast off whatever in this world we see doth hinder us from the holy fellowship of Christ Jesus; and strengthen us that we may be faithful to the end, that so we may obtain the Crown of life in that glory, where this noble *Galeacius* and all the heavenly host of Gods Saints do wait for us: *Amen.* This was his life, this was his end; let thy life be like his, and thy heart walk in the same way; then shall thy soul dye his death, and thy latter end shall be like his.

O Lord how glorious art thou in thy Saints.

www.ingramcontent.com/pod-product-compliance
Lightning Source LLC
Chambersburg PA
CBHW020304170426
43202CB00008B/488